POETIC VOYAGES
EAST SUSSEX

Edited by Alison Dowse

First published in Great Britain in 2001 by
YOUNG WRITERS
Remus House,
Coltsfoot Drive,
Peterborough, PE2 9JX
Telephone (01733) 890066

HB ISBN 0 75433 132 6
SB ISBN 0 75433 133 4

FOREWORD

Young Writers was established in 1991 with the aim to promote creative writing in children, to make reading and writing poetry fun.

This year once again, proved to be a tremendous success with over 88,000 entries received nationwide.

The Poetic Voyages competition has shown us the high standard of work and effort that children are capable of today. It is a reflection of the teaching skills in schools, the enthusiasm and creativity they have injected into their pupils shines clearly within this anthology.

The task of selecting poems was therefore a difficult one but nevertheless, an enjoyable experience. We hope you are as pleased with the final selection in *Poetic Voyages East Sussex* as we are.

CONTENTS

Herne Junior School

Iford & Kingston Primary School

Little Common School

Abbi Redman	67
Anna Walter	68
Lauren Plimmer	68
Vicky Cooper	69
Cara Gooch	69
Alice Scotcher	70
Jamie Leonard	70
Lauren Black	71
Tana Isted	72
Shanna Jeans	72
Rebecca Barrie	73
Elizabeth Francis	73
Lucy Killick	74
Jasmin Luck	74
Alex Vincent	75
Rae Gill	75
Jessie Francis	76

Meeching Valley Primary School

Fern Kearley	76
Chris McPherson	77
Chloe Ware	77
Charlotte Browlett	78
Katie Gibbs	78
Laura Farley	78
Darren Farrant	79
Callum Moore	79
Aaron Tubb	80
Lauren Seymour-Steed	80
Hollie Groucutt	81

Ninfield C of E School

Steven Franks	81
Tony Borrell	82
Nicholas Mayes	82
Marisa Reid	83
Mark Sayer	83
Charlotte Cannon	84

Elena Matthews	84
Danny Austin	85
Leah Allen	86
Poppy Anderson	86
James Freeman	87
Peter Davies	87
Nick Coughlan	88
Joeley Elphick	88

Park Mead CP School

Laura Chaplin	89
Jade Chittenden	89
Eleanor Risbridger	90
Emily Dann	90

Peasmarsh C of E Primary School

Siobhan Zysemil	91
Ricky Piggott	91
Tyler Watson	92
Terry Page	92
Samantha Richards	92
Danny Walton	93
Chrissie Wall	93
Felicity Barnes	94
Philippa Dunn	94
Katie Thomas	95
Leoni Ennis	95
Luke Sothcott	96
Ben Baker	96
Kirsty Juden	97
Jade Bull	97
Danielle Watts	98
Donna-Marie Maplesden	98
Jessica Beale	99
William Henry Nye	99
Thomas Martin	100
Callum Laverton	100
Matthew Saunders	101

Shinewater Primary School

Abby Higgins	136
Jason Akehurst	137
Lauren Hines	137
Craig Badcock	138
Joe Buckwell	138
Connor Feeney	139
Jimmy Kiteley	139
Kayleigh Fernie	140
Sami-Lea Perkins	140
Peter Gould	141
Jamie Wright	141
Kheva King	142

Stone Cross School

Jade Kearney	142
Suzanna Napper-Page	143
Lloyd Francis	143
Victoria Ball	144
Georgina Haffenden	144
Matthew Golledge	145
Thomas Sharp	146
Aimeé Read	146
Jamie Segwagwe	147
Caitlin Rowson	148
Jonathan Riches	149
Craig Bartlett	150
Stephanie Tween	151
Jack Davies	152
Liam Hughes	153
Natasha Henson	154
Jasmine Redfern	155
Joanne Mitchell	156
Zoe McCue	157
Ryan-Neil Linley	158
Ben Boobier	159
Jack Kenward	159
Matthew Winter	160

The Poems

FOOD

It's mushy
It's crunchy
It's cold or it's hot
It's good for you,
It's bad for you
I hear that a lot.
Mmm it's lovely,
Eerr it's yucky
I'm not eating that,
That can go to the dog or the cat.
It's sweet
It's sour
It's food.
Mmm.

Tom Carey (11)
Blacklands School

DOGS

They're hairy
They're scary
They're big and they're bold,
They're cute, they're cuddly
So I'm told.
They bark
They're dark
But sometimes brown,
They're hairy
They're scary
They're dogs.
Woof!

Daniel Rozier (10)
Blacklands School

THE FOUR SEASONS

Daffodils sprouting
Mums shouting
Spring clean
Make it be seen
That's the beginning of spring.

Oceans of the seas
Sailors sailing free
While kids are splashing
Ducks are quacking
That's a hot summer's day.

Leaves on the ground
While some animals sleep sound
Conkers cracking
Children clapping
That's a typical autumn's day.

Snow is laid
Snowballs are made
Gloves and scarves are worn
When Jesus was born
That's the cold winter's dawn.

Tara Hatfield (11)
Blacklands School

THE HORRIBLE DAY

The day is horrible and the fog is here.
No children are playing because the rain is near.

I want to find something good to do,
But the rain has flooded my toy-room too.

The electricity has gone and the mist is here,
So I lay down quietly and let all disappear.

I then woke up jumped in the air
And to all my delight the snow was there.

Jermaine Woods (8)
Blacklands School

MY BEST FRIEND SARAH

My best friend Sarah
Makes me laugh,
As she sings in the bath.

My best friend Sarah
Is as thin as a tin,
But not very dim.

My best friend Sarah
Has got a best band 5ive
And she goes to see them live.

My best friend Sarah
Is as red as a rose
But never ever likes to pose.

My best friend Sarah
Is as happy as a hippo
And always likes to disco.

My best friend Sarah
Is as fast as a Ferrari
And wants to go on a safari.

Parisa Aynehchian (11)
Blacklands School

CATS

I feel so lucky, I feel so free,
I can stay out all night and come back in the morning!
My owners feed me salmon and trout.
As I savour my meal I think to myself what's for pud?
I hate water it's so plain and boring.
Human beings have baths in water, drink water and use water in food.
And anyway, who wants to have something that's fallen from
                                        the sky in their belly?
Not me that's for sure!
I can lie on the sofa and watch the telly!
I can lie on the stairs and get in the way!
I can play with my toys,
Or I can go to sleep.
What a life of bliss for me!

Cassie Mackenzie (10)
Blacklands School

THE BEAR

The bear, the bear,
He has fuzzy brown hair,
He thumps through the woods
And collects goods,
That campers drop,
Among their crop,
The bear goes back to his cave
And there he'll be brave.

Charli Stagg (9)
Blacklands School

NUMBERS

On Saturday and Sunday I tried my best,
To get my times tables in my head.
But on Monday when I was asked a sum,
My mind went blank, I just acted dumb.
'What is 4x4?' the teacher asks.
It must be 8, oh no that's daft.
5x5 and 6x6,
Numbers, numbers they make me sick.
9x9 and 10x10,
I think I'm going round the bend.
All week long I try my best,
I really want to pass the test.
I just can't get numbers into my brain,
Next weekend I'll try again.

Johnathan Peters (11)
Blacklands School

SPACE QUEST

If I were a spaceman
Exploring Mars' hot crust,
I'd travel in my spaceship to
Find the famous space dust!
I'd walk the moon's grey craters
And dig for treasure on Mars,
While studying a flying comet,
I'd catch some shooting stars!
I would love to spin round
Saturn's ring on a beautiful clear night
And head towards Venus with
The help of the sun's bright light!

Stephanie Hartman (10)
Blacklands School

ANIMALS

It was in a jungle where the sun shines,
While a beaver was eating on its pines,
Wild birds were calling,
And monkeys were falling.

It was on a beautiful sandy beach,
Where no horrible teachers teach,
And in the sea, blue bottle-nosed dolphins swim,
While someone had found a quiet calm.

It was at night in a dark misty house,
Where nothing scrabbled about except for a mouse,
But something was sleeping on the landing, a dog,
Outside in the sty lived a very happy and lively hog.

It was out in the cold and gloomy farm,
Where someone held a hedgehog in their palm,
Also where a crazy horse lived in a warm stable,
While a mischievous cat was eating smelly food on the table.

It was in the woods where trees were glistening,
While squirrels were rustling and people were listening,
And where the rabbits were playing in the morning dew,
Also where the badgers had been, they left a clue.

It was at the riverside where the stream was flowing fast,
While giant leaping frogs listened to the stream as they passed,
And where baby otters buried their homes in the river bank,
And lovely bright fish jumped joyfully over the bridge plank.

It was in the sea where big blue whales live,
Also where fishermen collect shrimps in their sieve,
And where the seals where swimming smoothly through the water,
Cats were on a ship where suitcases were being carried by the porter.

Victoria Goldsmith (10)
Blacklands School

THE SEASON FAMILY

The king of winter watches the world,
As time grows old,
Winter's fingers reach up high,
As the birds fly by.
Flowers sleep through the land,
Waiting for the sun's warm hand.

The queen of spring tends to the flowers,
As the day passes by in hours,
As the flowers wake,
In the queen's quake.
Summer is soon to come,
With the warming of the sun,
But children pick the flowers,
Which took the queen so many hours.

The princess of summer keeps the rain away,
With the help of the sun's rays.
The baby lambs nose up to their mothers,
While they play with the others.
Children laugh and play,
Being ever so gay.
When summer dies,
She will sleepily lie.

The prince of autumn spreads his leaves,
As happy as can be.
Autumn hopes to be king,
But he never does ring,
Now all there is to do,
Is wait for it to start all over again.

Nicole Pavitt (9)
Blacklands School

CATS

Cats are furry,
Cats are nice,
Cats are beautiful,
They chase mice.

Round the living room floor,
In and out the doors,
Up and down the stairs,
Around all the chairs.

After a while they got dizzy
And decided to have a drink of fizzy,
After that they had a nap
Before they went to play snap.

Time has come to say goodnight,
Before they get a great big fright.

Mary Avery & Zoe Wallace (10)
Blacklands School

THE SUN IS SHINING

The sun is shining,
and the sky is blue.
The birds are singing,
and I am too.

The people are taking their
dogs for walks.
One's going round their
friend's house to talk.

I'm walking with my mum and dad,
We're going to the park,
I'm going to have so much fun,
We're staying till it's dark.

It's time to go home now,
Time to go to bed,
Brush your teeth and kiss your mum,
Rest your sleepy head.

Samantha Downey (9)
Blacklands School

AUTUMN

The beautiful tree, dancing in the wind,
Its leaves rustling, the trunk swaying,
The waving branches touching the sky,
Birds nesting in the knobbly boughs.

Squirrels burying their nuts for winter,
Autumn leaves scattered all over,
Baby squirrels running up and down,
Squirrels soaring through the air.

The dashing birds tweet and sing,
The squirrels crawl and scratch,
The children stare and listen,
To the birds and squirrels playing.

The beautiful tree, swinging in the wind,
Its leaves rustling, the trunk swaying,
The waving branches touching the sky,
Birds nesting in the knobbly boughs.

Chelsea Brunton (10)
Blacklands School

FANTASY SPACE

My ship capsized,
when it clashed with a rock.
Forget about astronomy,
it's space which had been locked.
Red, yellow, green and blue,
the colours are so clear.
If you look through a telescope,
the North Star is near.
As I sail around the sky,
looking for a sign.
Mars, Jupiter, mercury,
but not a star to climb.
A shimmering light,
is a star with a knock.
But this is a secret,
now we have to put it on a lock.

Rosie Tipler & Christie Phillips (9)
Blacklands School

HAPPY TIMES

S   chool is where I go each day
C   os it's where I learn and play
H   appy times with all my chums
O   n Mondays is when I do my sums
O   h the clock does tick so slow
L   unchtime bell,
        Time to go.
        Yum, yum.

Guy Standen (11)
Blacklands School

MY SUNNY DAY AT THE BEACH

I went to the beach,
With my bucket and spade,
I found a nice spot,
To sit in the shade.

I looked at the sea,
It was calm and clear.
It stretched for miles,
I could see the pier.

Everywhere I looked,
People were having fun,
Playing with beach-balls,
And building sandcastles in the sun.

Down by the waves,
I could see some shells,
All shapes and sizes,
Some looked like little bells.

I waded past the shells,
To swim in the sea.
What a lovely day,
This turned out to be.

I bought an ice cream,
That looked like shaving foam,
The sun had gone,
It was time to go home.

Keira Donnelly (11)
Blacklands School

IN THE JUNGLE

Down in the jungle where nobody goes,
There is a frightening place where everything grows.
The mangled trees stretch up so high,
It looks as if they are touching the sky.

The creepy silence is broken by a sound,
Like something crashing right through the ground.
A waterfall is thundering over some rocks,
And in the corner are some very large crocs.

Their beady eyes staring straight ahead,
Their mouths open wide as if they are dead!
The noisy monkeys swim all over the place,
They look like they're having a very fast race.

A huge spotted cat with large paws,
Is prowling through the jungle as he roars.
Now the light is fading, the night is drawing in,
The animals inside this place are all asleep within.

Down in the jungle where everyone should go.
Is a wonderful place that is worth getting to know.

Adéle Cook   (10)
Blacklands School

WALKING IN THE PARK

Walking in the park,
When it's cold and dark,
Movements in the night,
Give me such a fright.

Shadows in the trees,
Moving in the breeze,
Everything is quiet,
Except my knocking knees.

How I long for home,
When I'm all alone,
Walking in the park,
When it's cold and dark.

Maya Jenkins & Domi Hoath (11)
Blacklands School

POOR LITTLE HAMSTER!

Why am I here in this house?
I feel like I'm a mouse.

I am trapped, I want to be free,
I would like it better to live in a tree.

Please, please help me if you're out there,
Let me out, it's not fair.

I hate this cage so let me out,
I want to play out and about.

My fur is dirty and cold,
My food I can't hold,
Because it's started to mould.

The nuts are like jelly,
The seeds feel horrible in my belly,
So now I'm smelly.

Jessica Faisey (10)
Blacklands School

THE MOON HAIKU

Sunny, bright, silver.
Bumpy, lumpy, huge round ball.
Shining through the night.

Jeremy Martin (9)
Bourne County Primary School

STARS HAIKU

Black sky, small circles.
Sun is yellow and bursting.
Stars up in the sky.

Menila Braho (10)
Bourne County Primary School

EARTH'S TWIN HAIKU

We're zooming through space,
Seeking, searching for Earth's twin,
Because Earth's melted.

Daniel Bowles (9) & Joshua Smith (10)
Bourne County Primary School

THE MOON HAIKU

A cat's eye glowing
and a gob-stopper floating.
It's a crystal ball.

Charley Mulhern (10)
Bourne County Primary School

The Visitors From Infinity And Beyond

The aliens,
Secretive, inexplicable,
Surprising, haunting, teasing
Mysterious visitors from outer space,
Extraterrestrials.

Leon Tucker (9)
Bourne County Primary School

Stars Haiku

White, bright, glittering,
Millions sparkling away,
Small in the night sky.

Peter Humphries (9)
Bourne County Primary School

The Sun Haiku

The sun is a star.
Shines in the beautiful sky.
In the shining sky.

Rebekah Clark (9)
Bourne County Primary School

The Stars Haiku

Twinkling in the dark
Shining in the black dark night
Sky glowing up high.

Damien White (9)
Bourne County Primary School

A Corner Of The Artist's Room

I imagine the quiet
As she sits in the corner of the room
Thinking of the outside world;
The walls as yellow as daffodils,
With a triangular shadow printed on the wall,
With a wooden chair in the dark corner,
A blue shawl hanging over the corner of the chair,
And a parasol leaning against it.
The desk under the window,
On the window there are cream curtains,
But where has the artist gone?

Amy Kay (9)
Bourne County Primary School

The Rocket Haiku

It flies like a bird
Shining in the sky so high
Super speed missile.

Nathan Williams (9)
Bourne County Primary School

The Moving Planet

Planets
Gigantic spherical
Spinning, flying, whirling,
Stretching away from each other
Solar system.

Adam Daubeney (10)
Bourne County Primary School

ROOM

In the corner of the room I see
A vase of colourful flowers,
Yellow walls and table and chairs,
A long blue shawl with a cream parasol,
Leaning on the arm of the cane chair,
And how quiet it is
Without her there!
Where has she gone?

Bethan Kay (9)
Bourne County Primary School

BRIGHT LIGHTS

Stars
Glassy, galaxies
Shining, tingling, bright things
Lovely to look at
Milky way.

Matthew Ab (10)
Bourne County Primary School

STARS HAIKU

A large hot white ball
Twinkling in the bright night sky
Like a small fire fly.

Christopher Winter (9)
Bourne County Primary School

THE STARS

The stars
Sparkling, whirling
Shooting losing sparkles,
Blazing away in the sky,
Galaxy.

Andrew Lower (9)
Bourne County Primary School

STARS

Stars
Sparkly and bright
Glittering, shining and shooting,
Making pictures
Galaxy.

Stacie-Louise Richardson (10)
Bourne County Primary School

SATURN

Saturn,
Multi-coloured, bright,
Spinning, changing, shining,
Twirling into deeper space,
Gigantic.

Hiu-Yan Chow (10)
Bourne County Primary School

THE SUN

It's bright and white
Twinkling, shining, brightening
All over the galaxy
Beyond.

Keely Kelleher (9)
Bourne County Primary School

THE TRAVELLING SPIDER

The spider travelled far and wide
Searching for a place to hide
The journey took an hour or two
Just to hide away from you.

Why she hides I do not know
Maybe just to have a go
At spinning a web or making a nest
And eating bugs in lemon zest.

Through the country or sand dunes
And on the way hears wonderful tunes
At the end her poor legs ached
But she only went to see her mate.

Who lived a million miles away
You'd be lucky to get there in a day
Why she went you'd have to find out
Maybe just to walk about.

Along the wonderful bright green fields
Or swim in the sea with small grey seals
Not a tempting thing to do
Especially for a spider.

Lucie Martlew (10)
Brede Primary School

WEATHER JOURNEY

Like a rainbow
After showers
Special people
Brighten hours.

Like the sun
After a storm
Makes you feel
All glowy and warm.

The snow so clean
Crispy and white
Makes you shiver
With excitement
And delight.

The wind blows the leaves
From the trees to the ground
They go in circles
Around and around.

The clouds so grey
On a rainy day
When the sky is blue
There's no colour in view.

Autumn, summer, winter and spring
Do you know what each season brings?

Charlotte Hughes (11)
Brede Primary School

THE SPIDER WHO FLEW

As I journey above the world
Up amongst the clouds
My tiny eight legs curled
My hairy body shivers faintly
Soaring above the snow-capped mountains
I roll my eyes daintily
Over the everlasting blue-green sea
Watch the fields of tropical vegetation
Pass under me
The sun sets under an unknown land
An amazing experience
Mile upon mile of golden sand
As I see untouched earth
Houses here and there
See where cities had their birth
Fly higher than a spiralling bird
Follow the path of a plane
It's a miracle and quite absurd
I know I'll never do this again
I'm a special creature
Surprisingly I can fly
Graciously whirling and twirling
As I travel through the sapphire sky
I watch the world's splendours miraculously unfurl
I've had a charming life
A spider who was a privileged girl
My unique wings fold away
Down, down I rapidly descend
This is the finale of my last day
My life has come to an abrupt end.

Louise Loveless (11)
Brede Primary School

REMEMBRANCE

I can't help holding on,
Yet I know thee will not come back,
Inside, my heart is full of hope
But the outside is dismal and black.

Gone from thy arms I may be,
But you will stay,
In my heart and always shall,
Forevermore and a day.

All the sombre trails of the world,
I seem to walk across,
A magnet to unhappiness I seem to be,
From tip of toe to root of hair.

Although your stone of remembrance,
'Tis still a comfort to me,
'Tis not as comforting as thou thy self,
Or to know that here is thee.

I can't help holding on,
Yet I know thee will not come back,
Inside my heart is full of hope,
But the outside is dismal and black.

Jessica Butler (10)
Burwash C of E Primary School

THE MOON

The moon comes up every night,
To let the people see,
But in the morning it has disappeared,
I wonder where it could be?

Jessica Shale (9)
Burwash C of E Primary School

22

BRIGHTON SENSORY

Stinky fish on the market,
Fish and chips smelling good,
Salt in the sea lapping away
Sailing through the leaves.

Spy the West Pier and the Palace Pier,
Entertainment all around,
Shops, hotels and restaurants,
Lights all twinkling pretty and bright.

Listen to the sea crash banging on the beach,
Music playing dance and jig,
Amusements playing loud and clear,
Come and play, dance and cheer.

Come and feel the soft light breeze
Or the rough and tumble wind,
Taste and feel the salt from the sea,
Spray flying from the shore.

Claire Barden (11)
Burwash C of E Primary School

BRIGHTON SENSORY POEM

I could taste the salty spray; it swept across the stony beach
As if it was trying to wash the whole town away,
I could see the waves crashing against the hard concrete wall
As if they were trying to break it open,
I could feel the wind pushing against me like it blows a leaf in the sky.
I could hear the birds squawking in the sky
As if a predator was chasing them,
I could smell the salty fish from the sea
As if it were a fish and chip shop.

Constance Alderson Blench (11)
Burwash C of E Primary School

THEY'RE GONE

Why do people have to go?
People miss them loads and loads,
They're hurt inside,
They'll talk and cry.

Even if you're not too close,
You'll still cry,
Those tears which run down faces,
All those red patches round their eyes.

Deep down inside,
Their hearts are broken,
Whenever they hear that name,
It'll remind them of that day.

They didn't mean to make people cry,
To make people feel so bad,
They say to themselves 'Why did this happen?'
You've got to let go.

Don't worry,
They're not gone,
They're right by your side,
Stop worrying about them.

They've gone to a better place.

Elizabeth Gudgeon (10)
Burwash C of E Primary School

IN MY HEAD

In my head
There is a picture of the past
That has gone.
There is a raging war trying to destroy
My brain.

In my head
There is a volcano trying to burst out
There is a lonely feeling
As if I am falling
Off a gigantic cliff.

Christopher Bright (8)
Charters Ancaster College

SECRETS OF SPRING

Through the door I can see
A lamb skipping up and down in the field,
A butterfly hovering in the spring air.

Through the door I can see
A nest cradling two new eggs,
Lots of bluebells growing down the lane.

Through the door I can see
Fresh sparkling dew on the green grass,
Lots of birds waking up to spring.

Through the door I can see
Bright pink blossom fluttering in the air,
Fat little bumble bees gathering pollen.

Through the door I can see
Daffodils bursting out of their buds,
New-born foals grazing in the meadows.

Go on, open the door,
See spring for yourself!

Eden Richards (8)
Charters Ancaster College

IN MY HEAD

In my head
There is a raging storm trying to get me
There are calm peaceful waves
Splashing against the grey, rough rocks
There is the flickering memory
Of my family.

In my head
There are some bubbly hearts
Floating, popping now and then.
There is a violent thunderstorm
Shocking my brain
There is a flowing river waiting
To flood.

In my head
There is a golden pendulum
Swinging back and forth.
There is a memory
Stabbing at my brain
Scorching and blazing
Taking all in its path.

Jahna Drunis (10)
Charters Ancaster College

THE SPRING

Through the window I can see
Bits of coloured blossom swaying on a green tree,
Little ducks quacking in a slimy green pond.

Through the window I can see
Woodpeckers pecking at a green tree covered with blossom,
Orange buds shining brightly in the sun.

Through the window I can hear
Children playing noisily in the garden filled with flowers,
The soft neighing of the foals nuzzling their mothers.

Through the window I can see
A burning sun beating down on me,
So go on, open the window and take a good look.

Chloe Smith (8)
Charters Ancaster College

IN MY HEAD

In my head
There is a delighted jack-in-the-box
Springing.
There is a family frame
Of memories.

In my head
There is a violin playing
Peaceful music.
There is a prickly knife
Stabbing at my temple.

In my head
There is a bomb
Pushing out bad words.
There is a thunderstorm
Crushing and destroying me.

Brittany Mayes (9)
Charters Ancaster College

SHOPPING CENTRE

There are thousands of shops
Millions of feet
All walking and talking
Crying and buying, selling and yelling
Pulling and pushing, rattling and prattling
Burning and churning and yearning
To buy!
Shoes are shining, people dining.
Muttering and tutting, moaning and groaning
Mumbling and jumbling
Chanting songs, planting seeds.
Chewing and gluing
Making and baking, savouring and flavouring
Tills springing and pinging
They want to buy!

Rosalyn Putland (9)
Charters Ancaster College

ELEMENTS

The moon is a floating world of dust,
A hopeless planet
That dances around
The earth.

Fire like a red and yellow mass
Of dancing, dangerous flames.
A monster waiting
To kill.

The sea is gentle, lapping, rippling
Army of water
That is ready to storm the land
Waiting to attack
In a fierce battle.

But ice is like a mirror
A colourless copycat of glass
A new twin
A perfect friend.

Alexander Houlbrook (9)
Charters Ancaster College

IN MY HEAD

In my head
There is a calm dream floating.
There is a scorching devil
Drilling at my brain.

In my head
There is a cliff pushing boulders
Off the edge.
There is a bomb ticking.

In my head
There is a volcano
Destroying everything in its path.
There is a parade stamping
And lightning hitting
Everything.

Alexander Hazell (8)
Charters Ancaster College

AT THE BUILDING SITE

Jumbling and rumbling
Vroom, vroom
It's drilling and thundering
Smashing and dashing
Thrashing and vibrating
Boom, boom.
Falling and crying
Smoking to ash
Destroying, springing and lifting
Falling back down, pushing and pulling.
'Snap' goes the wood
sawdust flying, sawing and hitting.
'Bang' light goes to dark
the crowd disappearing
there is something shining
. . . A one pound coin.

Frances Gray (9)
Charters Ancaster College

SPRINGTIME

Through the door
Are baby lambs frisking about the sheep
Are daffodils poking their heads from the sleepy ground,
Is a blue and white sky with a big circle of yellow,
Is the scent of sweet smelling grass,
Are trees with blossom dotted here and there waving in the breeze,
Go on, open the door!

Rebecca Stewart-Hodgson (8)
Charters Ancaster College

AT NIGHT

The moon looks like
A chocolate chip cookie or
A banana all curved.
It lights up the world
Like a torch.
It shines at night on the sea
Which is sometimes like a monster
Crashing on the beach.
The storms make it angry and violent
Gobbling up fishermen.
But it is sometimes calm
And there is sand between my toes.

Mollie Alcott (9)
Charters Ancaster College

SUN AND SKY

A red hot piece
Of fire.
A round white ball
That shines in the sky
And glitters and glows
With the stars.

A warm piece of blue
That is going to
Splash all over me.
At night it is as if
A man pours
Black oil all over the sky
And in the daytime
He sucks it back up.

Greg Holden (8)
Charters Ancaster College

IN MY HEAD

In my head there is a
Raging fire burning
Waiting, waiting for my enemies to come.
There is thunder crashing
And lightning flashing.
There is sadness turning into joy
At the sight of people I know.

In my head there is an
Inquiring question mark
Wanting a chance to say.
There is a land of milk and honey
Where people dance and sing.
There is a person in a small dark house
On a lonely hill
Waiting for someone to visit
But . . . no one will.

In my head there is
Violence when thunder and lightning meet
But there is also
The calm, peaceful sea
With nothing to disturb the surface
But a yacht.

Jessica Collishaw (10)
Charters Ancaster College

IN MY HEAD

In my head
There is a tidal wave
Causing destruction and turning the world
Into its oyster
Until it is a puddle
On the dark floor
Of space.

In my head
There is a dagger stabbing at my brain
There is a violent storm
Destroying all the peaceful calm.

In my head
There is a demon of meanness
Waiting for me.
There is a clock tower
Reminding me of home.

In my head
There is a tall figure
Rising from the darkness
There is a question mark
Wanting answers.

In my head
There is a generous, kind part of my mind
There is a part consumed by love and emotion
But there is
A thunderstorm corrupting my dreams.

William Adams (9)
Charters Ancaster College

THE FIRE

The fire is a warm greeting to you
Its body is a warm atmosphere all around you.
The flickering flames engulf the chimney
Calm and whimpering it slowly dies away
It starts hissing softly like a snake in pain

Flaming triumphantly the smoke expands
Crackling and slashing it starts whipping the air
Screaming and shuddering it pounces like a tiger.
After sparkling and gleaming like a thousand children
The fire is finally finished.
It looks like a bouquet of glittering sparks
Coming down at you like a thousand knives.

Madison Walters (10)
Dallington Primary School

THE WEATHER

The weather is a temperamental child
Sometimes, screaming in anger
Whipping up the wind and whisking the waves
Pounding on the earth as if it were his battered pillow
Howling and shrieking in fury.

But sometimes, laughing and ready to play
Gently fanning the breeze and stroking the water
Smiling on the earth from a high blue ceiling
Laughing, and wanting to join us.

Henry Nathan (11)
Dallington Primary School

WATER

The water is a horse raging in her fury
Waving up the water in her pain
She smacks her mane against the shore
As she cries for help in pain
As she smashes up the pebbles and rocks
And she dives back into the sea
Splashing like an egg spitting in the pan.

The horse roars in the deep
And splashes in the shallows
She destroys everything in her path
Ripping the seaweed and turning rocks to ash.
She starts to yawn and whimper
Her head hits the ground
And she falls asleep.

Adam Brown (9)
Dallington Primary School

WATER

Water is a raindrop coming down the window
It is a stream flowing with water
A tap with water dripping down the drain
It is the sea lapping over the shore
Like a bird singing its own song.
Water is a strong flowing river
It is a bath ready for someone to get in
It is a glass of water ready to be drunk
Like a horse galloping down your throat.
It is a stream leading to a great ocean.

Rose Kinloch-Haken (9)
Dallington Primary School

THE WIND

The wind is a mad bloodhound
Leaping and jumping, ripping washing off the line
He howls and playfully chases children
He jumps on roofs and rips tiles down.

The wind is a gentle girl
She calmly blows
Rippling the sea as the children splash
The wind breathes a breeze.

The wind is filled with anger
He is full of rain
It is rough and tumble, like a wrestler
As he screeches and lets out his anger.

Once again, the wind is gentle
And sends a breeze through the trees.

Gina Baker (10)
Dallington Primary School

THE FIRE

The fire is an angel dancing with joy,
Burning anything in its way.
The smoke is my mums burning toast,
It turns into fast approaching rain clouds.
The wood is bacon and eggs sizzling in a pan.
The fire is hotter than red hot chillies in a curry,
The smoke is a smoker having his pipe and keeping on filling it up,
The fire is thousands of babies crying for milk.

Louke Van Der Meer (10)
Dallington Primary School

FOG

The fog is a ghost swimming in the air.
It is cold and unloved
The fog is the enemy creeping towards you
The fog is the Titanic, dead, white, withered.
The fog is cold, taking over every sense in your body.
It starts at the feet
Numbing them into a deep sleep
Next your body
Faster and faster
It won't stop.
Now your head is drowning in whiteness
The mist is attacking you from all angles
Stabbing you with a thousand knives.
The fog lets out a wild shriek as if it is dying.
You feel life coming back to your body.
Warmth spreading through the world.

Alix Thompson (10)
Dallington Primary School

WEATHER

The weather is a giant hand
Lying over the world like a snowy blanket.

The weather is a spot of rain,
Dripping like the tear of a dog that has just left its mother.
The weather is like a bursting flower
It is unexpected.

Harriet White (9)
Dallington Primary School

WIND

Wind is like a chariot flying through the morning sky
The horses cried by the whipping of the ghost riders
The wind is like a whole army on horseback thrashing all around
The men on horseback screeching like a baby being born.
The wind whistles like a tidal wave
Crash.
The wind, wind, wind.

Josh Jackson (10)
Dallington Primary School

THE FOG

The fog is a giant ghost floating in the air
Thickening the atmosphere and engulfing the sky
Grabbing the trees and hiding them inside its mouth.
As night grows the ghost floats away
Then when morning comes it reveals itself once more.
When winter is over the sun grows stronger
And melts the fog into rain.

Ben Pattenden (10)
Dallington Primary School

FIRE

The fire is a constellation of stars
Sparkling in the dark night sky.
It is dancing angels leaping and jumping
The fire is a hissing cobra spitting at its prey
The fire is a tiger hiding in the long luscious grass
Waiting to pounce.

Jodie Sutherland (9)
Dallington Primary School

FIRE

The fire is a dancing angel
Sparkling in the night.
It is the sun spreading all over the world.
Like a thousand lights lit all in one house.
Fire is the danger of millions of people,
Snapping at anything it can find.
The fire . . . the fire . . . the fire.

Bryony Frost (10)
Dallington Primary School

FOG

The fog is a crystal white soldier creeping stealthily towards you
It swirls round the trees, choking their branches.
The fog horn sounds as a wolf howls in the night.
The fog is a ghost swallowing everything in its path.
The fog is a lifting bed sheet as it rises.
It is a translucent piece of paper just letting the light through.

Charlie Jones (11)
Dallington Primary School

FIRE

The fire is fog drifting around the sky
The flames are like hot pizzas burning in the oven.
Crackling sounds coming out like a witch cackling.
The fire keeps going as the sun crackles like fire itself
As it burns the air is getting all smoky and dusty
As the fire expands smoke fills the air.

Emma Weekes (11)
Dallington Primary School

THE MOON

The moon is a smiling face
Winking down at the earth.
It is a Ritz cracker that is half eaten.
It is a glass of lemonade
When it is all bubbly.
It is cheese with holes
As if a mouse has eaten through it.

The moon shines down on the earth
As if it is a lump of gold
Lighting Earth's darkness
So light as if the morning has already dawned.

Kate Baker (10)
Dallington Primary School

THE SNOW

The snow is a gigantic cloth covering the luxurious plains
As it tries to cover the world forever.
While on the highest mountain there is a catastrophic ice shift
As if there is a person moving the cloth
To block even the bravest mountain climbers.

Matthew Frei (10)
Dallington Primary School

FIRE

Fire is the roaring tiger ready to pounce
Teasing his prey flickering in and out of the glowing embers
Moving as quick as light
Crackling and spitting as it charges
And darting in and out.

The fire is a glowing star
Shining brighter than anything in the darkening sky
Shimmering and shining, glittering and glowing
Dying, dying, dying away.

Abby Corliss (11)
Dallington Primary School

THE FIRE

The fire looks like thousands of dancers
It feels like thousands of knives in your body
The air is so hot it feels like your snugly bed.
It crackles on the leaves in the wood being trodden on.
It looks like thousands of vicious faces
It feels like hands clinging on to you
So hard that it burns your skin.
There is no air left to breathe.

Deborah Blanch (10)
Dallington Primary School

SNOW

The snow is a fallen cloud
Scattered all over the woods
Soft and bouncy as children play snowballs.
The snow is a feather falling
As it falls lightly on my cheek and tingles my neck.
The sun shines on the snow
Like a thousand crystals in the sunlight.
The snow is a sheep, fluffy and white
It sits in the sun all day
At the end of the day it is gone.

Hannah Kinloch-Haken (9)
Dallington Primary School

THE WATER

The water is an unknown animal
Which creeps down streams and crunches the stone.
This makes your senses stir.
When you put your feet in the water
You get a static sensation
As if you have been frozen for a hundred years.

The water is an unknown animal
Which creeps down streams and crunches the stone.
This makes your senses stir.
When you put your feet in the water
You get a welcoming feel
As if you were in bed next to a fire.

Ben Harris (10)
Dallington Primary School

THE FIRE BEAST

Fire is a roaring beast
Being awoken from his den.
He roars and growls
Like two dogs having a scrap.

He moves this way and that
As though the two dogs are going round each other.
Now the beast,
Very confused,
Goes to his den
Not wanting to be awoken again.

James Price (10)
Dallington Primary School

JOURNEY TO MARS

As
I walk
To the lift
My guts and
Bravery go
Adrift. When I look
Up at the space ship
I look down and begin
To hate   it. As I
Come to   the door
My eyes   look up
From the floor. When
They lock me up all tight
I think of the risks on this
Flight. As I sit in the chair
The tension is too hard to
Bare. As the rocket begins
To fire my head and stomach
Feel quite dire. As I head for
Planet Mars I think of all the
Other stars. One year has gone
I'm just about there but
Something's gone wrong. I
Shout in despair. It's fixed
And alright. I made it on
This very daring flight.

Mark Cranfield (11)
Framfield C of E School

JOURNEY OF A TURTLE

J   ust along the shore mother turtle lays her eggs.
O   n the wet sand the eggs lay like tiny gem stones.
U   nderneath the shells the baby turtle starts to grow.
R   eady are the eggs to hatch and open.
N   ow all the eggs have hatched.
E   veryone must take its chance to get to the sea.
Y   et each one faces a dangerous challenge to the sea.

O   ver head the birds start to circle.
F   rom high up in the air they look like tiny dots.

A   ll the time they are moving closer to the sea.

T   he turtles are almost at the ocean edge.
U   nderneath the waves they will be safe.
R   olling bracers will pull them under.
T   he few that made it are safe now.
L   ots are lost to birds and fish on the way.
E   ach one safe in the sea to grow bigger.

Matthew Reed (10)
Framfield C of E School

MY NAME IS . . .

My name is Couldn't Care Less,
Let the rhinos die.
My name is Can't Be Bothered,
Why should I?

My name is Go Away,
Just let the oil spill.
My name is Bother Someone Else,
Only a few birds it will kill.

My name is Let The Forest Die,
And the animals fry.
My name is Haven't Got The Time,
I don't care about the holes in the sky.

My name is Care About The Environment,
Listen and help it not to die,
My name is Help The Animals,
We can all make a difference if we *try*.

Gemma Stanley (11)
Framfield C of E School

THE SWALLOW'S JOURNEY

T   he swallow goes on a long journey, he will see,
H   ippos,
E   lephants.

S   nakes,
W   ildebeests,
A   ntelope,
L   anaguor monkeys,
L   ions,
O   ver Africa they will fly
W   inging their way across the plains
S   aker falcons take their toll.

J   ourneys are dangerous
O   ld and young fall with exhaustion,
U   nder the waves they feebly flap,
R   ivers they cross,
N   ight time falls but they fly on
E   ngland they reach
Y   earning for food and rest.

Jamie Diplock (10)
Framfield C of E School

THE SNOWMAN'S JOURNEY

The snowman falls from the sky in pieces
Every day a child of his is born
Every day a child of his dies.
As the sun wakes in the open skies.

He is given a hat and a broom,
He stands stiff and tall as if on guard,
The snowman is built year after year,
Dreading the time when spring is here.

The snowman watches round his white kingdom,
Watches the road as cars whiz by,
The time when spring comes is near,
The snowman wants to keep his body here.

The snowman stares up at the light blue sky,
His face is sad.
To the houses all about 'Goodbye' he says.
Then he looks at his arms both going separate ways.

The snowman's arms are moving,
His nose is slipping too.
His eyes drop down to the ground,
Then he melts without making a sound.

Catherine Bush (10)
Framfield C of E School

THE OLD BARN

The old barn stands there, oldest of all
With its huge, big, crumbly walls.
It stands high, it stands tall
That's the barn, oldest of all.

The old barn stands there wide and crusty
On the floor inside it is dirty and dusty.
You would think that it would last
But in five hundred years it will just be evidence from the past.

Kellie Irwin (10)
Framfield C of E School

'ARE WE THERE YET?'

I hop in the back, that's where I sit,
Then I put my belt on, it always goes 'click!'
'Where are we going? Do we have to go far?'
It seems like I spend half my life in the car!

The engine starts, we're off on our way,
I think we're going to the beach today,
It should take an hour, the weather looks bleak,
When you're sat in the back it seems like a week!

The engine is humming, we're speeding along,
This can't last forever, something must go wrong!
The radio's blaring, we're singing a song,
'Is there far to go?' 'No it won't take long.'

The car starts slowing, it's beginning to rain,
Up ahead there's traffic, it's blocking our lane.
I look out the window, my heart fills with dread,
I see the sign 'Road Works Ahead!'

We wait and wait but don't get far,
It looks like we're spending all day in the car,
Dad says 'I'm fed up with this delay,
We will have to come back another day.'

Matthew Molloy (9)
Framfield C of E School

AN OTTER'S RIVER SWIM

Never stopping,
Never starting,
They like to catch
Fish and tickle
Their tummies.
They learn all this from
Their mummies.

Never stopping,
Never starting,
His flippers flip
His tail flops
He's never happy
He's never sad
He is always laughing though.

Otters dip, bob and glide
Swerve, jump and wiggle
Along the river side.
Never stopping,
Never starting.

They peer round corners
Swim through holes
Playing jokes and teasing
The voles.

This is the voyage
This is his life.

Charlotte Belton (10)
Framfield C of E School

OUT AND ABOUT

Some cars are red
Some bikes are blue
We have to go on a ride
Thanks to you.

Some planes are white
Some bushes are green
We're halfway there
Thanks to you.

Some motor bikes are black
Some go-karts are brown
We're there
Thanks to you.

Some trains are yellow
Some trams are orange
We're halfway back
Thanks to you.

Some helicopters are purple
Some boats are gold
We're back
Yippee!

Nathan Hobbs (9)
Framfield C of E School

JOURNEY OF A BABY BIRD

I am a little baby bird
Trying hard to fly.
I can reach the sky now
As I'm flying very high.

I can't see my mummy
She's flown too far,
I can hardly see anything
Oh look there's a car.
          Bang.

I'm in a back garden
My wings can't seem to flutter.
I can hear a noise now
Oh no it's a hedge cutter.
          Splat.

I'm in the paws of a cat now
Who has just sharpened his claws,
He looks very friendly
And now I'm in his jaws.

Ryan Clapham (10)
Framfield C of E School

IT'S SNOWING

Wake up! Wake up! It's snowing!
I'm going to make a snowball.
Get dressed, let's get going
My snowman will be really tall.

The snow is deep and even,
My footprints they stand out.
The air is cold to breath in
Snowballs are flying about.

We are cold, wet and happy,
When a snowball hits my face I blink.
Snowballs flying around slap me.
I want to go in for a hot milk drink.

Jacqueline Bush (8)
Framfield C of E School

HOLIDAYS

I went on holiday to Rye.
When I got there I ate an apple pie.

I went on holiday to France.
When I got there I started to dance.

I went on holiday to Spain.
When I got there the weather was rain!

I went on holiday to Greece.
When I got there it was too hot for a fleece.

I went on holiday to Wales.
When I got there it was full of frogs, slugs and snails.

I went on holiday to the Seychelles.
When I got there I smelt lots of strange smells.

I went on holiday to Japan.
When I got there I needed a fan.

I went on holiday to Peru.
When I got there I looked in the zoo.

Megan Hussey (8)
Framfield C of E School

ALONE

I sit all alone on the bus to nowhere,
This is a journey where you pay no fare.

We zoom past steep, snow-capped mountains,
Often we come across still, dried-up fountains.

We pass green fields of horses and cattle,
Under the bus I hear a blasting rattle.

I begin to feel tired and fall asleep,
When I awake I begin to weep.

I miss my family very, very much,
And Flopsy in her warm, cosy rabbit hutch.

I reach the land of joy and hope,
But without my family, I don't think I'll cope.

Holly Cowen (11)
Framfield C of E School

THE WHITE HORSE

Up the top of the hill,
Stood the white horse.
Very, very big,
And very, very old.
Lying in the wind
And never moving
He will stay forever.

Cameron Giles (9)
Framfield C of E School

MOON

The moon is the smell of fresh metallic
Just been minted from the factory.

It is the sound of a howling wolf
Echoing through the silent night.

It is a glowing lemon lolly
All crisp and new.

It is the touch of silky, powdery dust
All soft and crumbly.

It is the taste of powdery cheese
Slowly resting in my belly.

Claire Stott (11)
Herne Junior School

THE TREE

A tree is an enormous ogre
standing at the bottom of my garden.

Its branches, the bony hands
of witches grabbing out for you.

Its trunks, the rough skin
of a porcupine.

Yet when the world ruffles its hair
the leaves sing out like a lady.

Hannah Simpson (10)
Herne Junior School

VIOLENT VOLCANO

There the destructive, violent volcano,
Unhurriedly, formed over thousands and thousands of years,
Frequently violent, vicious and vast,
Like a vibrating earthquake shuddering the quaking Earth,
Like an uncontrolled river overflowing,
Rapidly it makes me feel so small,
Like a wild flea scurrying over a barking dog,
There the destructive violent volcano,
Hurtfully reminds us how vicious natural disasters can be.

Chloe Williams (11)
Herne Junior School

THE VOLCANO

Dangerously, the bubbling volcano
Erupts unexpectedly
Often destructive, sweltering. Towering
Like a pie quickly exploding
Like a giant topless mountain always bubbling
Now it makes me feel scared.
Like a dumb beetle spinning on its back.
Dangerously, the bubbling volcano
Reminds us of how short our life is.

Alex Gunn (10)
Herne Junior School

A HANDFUL OF HAIKUS

Cold, snowy morning,
Blackbirds singing endlessly,
Vast choir of angels.

Stars cover night sky,
Foxes scavenging for food,
Shadows on dark streets.

Siobhan Ransom (10)
Herne Junior School

GREAT WATERFALL

Steadily, the water flows
  Suddenly, the water drops
    Powerfully, it smashes the sharp rocks,
      Steamily, a mist of droplets appears
        Quickly, it continues over a rocky bed.

Craig Leeves (11)
Herne Junior School

THE VOLCANO

Powerful volcano,
Been around for millions of years,
Strong, powerful, fiery,
Like a pot full of fire.
Boiling hot treacle,
Ash like snow falling on me,
We like a helpless ant to a human,
The powerful volcano,
How hot will it get?

Rupert Lomax (11)
Herne Junior School

THE STORM

Its irritated body disturbingly trickled along the windowsill,
Its twangy voice whispered to the messy grass,
Its exasperated movement shook the trees with an indignant howl,
Its depressed feeling hassled the village cats who mewed with fear,
It hecticly threw the tiles off the roofs,
Its furious rage littered everywhere with the rubbish from the bins,
It flipped over five cars with its atrocious, vexed anger,
Its monstrous, infuriated temper lividly shook my bones that night.

Anna Scales (11)
Herne Junior School

MY BEDROOM

I lie in my bed; and look around
Grey and scary walls I've found
The paper's gone, the plaster's bare
All I can do is lay and stare.

Wishing hard as I close my eyes
That a fairy comes to hide the paint
So to cover the walls that I hate.
I know what!
Mum and Dad will have to paint.

Man United red and white
That's what I call pure delight.

Matthew Fayers (10)
Herne Junior School

THE ANCIENT WINDS OF EGYPT

The ancient winds of Egypt.
Silenced forever,
No pharaohs left to rule.
Now people love to see,
The ancient temples left for me.

John Parker (10)
Herne Junior School

THE SCORPION

Patiently, the scorpion awaits his prey
Gradually, he tenses his tail
Craftily, he flashes his eyes
Powerfully, he charges
Fatally, he stings the flesh.

Joshua Tunstill (10)
Herne Junior School

THE SNAKE

Smoothly the snake slithers,
Patiently watching to catch its prey.
Suddenly it spots movement,
Quietly it creeps under the sand.
Skilfully it appears next to the prey,
Speedily it widens its mouth.
Ferociously its mouth snaps down,
Rapidly the prey escapes.
Hungrily it moves on.

Kirsty Constable (11)
Herne Junior School

TIGER KENNING

Food-ripper
Royal-prancer
Claw-gripper
Stripe-striker
Ear-piercer
Shade-sleeper
Food-murderer
Ear-pointer
Grass-crawler
Pack-leader
Tongue-licker
Ear-twitcher
Jungle-creeper

Louise Gray (10)
Herne Junior School

FOOT

Sock-smeller
Shoe-eater
Ball-booter
Fast-grower
Bike-peddler
Shoe-wearer
Hot-runner
Tree-climber

Sam Coates (11)
Herne Junior School

TIGER CUB KENNING

Ball-prancer
Food-ripper
Clothes-tearer
Ear-piercer
Stripe-streaker
Bottle-sucker
Shade-sleeper
Meat-eater
Pin-poker
Grass-crawler
Ear-twitcher
Sun-bather
Keeper-liker.

Holly Robinson (11)
Herne Junior School

DOG

Tail-wagging
Voice-growling
Nose-sniffing
Ear-shaking
Saliva-dripping
Eye-blinking
Teeth-clenching
Leg-stretching
Claw-scraping
Tongue-licking
Dog

Chelsee Bennett (11)
Herne Junior School

THE CANDLE

At the end of the church,
Stands a perfumed lady,
Her hair crackles and spits.
Her waxy skin gleams golden.
She spits soapy water drops.

Sarah Newberry (10)
Herne Junior School

CLOUDS

Sky-wearer
Rain-producer
Thunder-maker
Fantasy-weaver
Lightning-flasher
Candy floss-softener
Pillow-pretender
Soft toy-imitator

Lucy Mahony (10)
Herne Junior School

A GLADIATOR

Think of the arena
Huge lion
Other gladiators man on man
One on one
A fight to the bloody end

Oliver Moffitt (10)
Herne Junior School

MY HOLIDAY IN CORNWALL

Softly I sleep in the caravan bed,
Like a hedgehog in its hibernation,
Playfully I swim in the swimming pool,
Like a fish being caught on a fishing rod,
Excitedly I win a competition,
Like an athlete winning a medal,
Quietly I feed the ducks,
Like a bird feeding its young,
Happily I play in the sand,
Beautifully the sun is shining,
Glimmering sea that shines so blue,
Noisily the children play,
Peacefully the fish swim in the sea,
Sadly I have to go home!

Lisa Newberry (10)
Herne Junior School

FUNNY FACES

Have you ever looked up to the sky
And asked the question why?

All those funny faces
Appear in the most strangest places.

There are bits of blue and bits of white
And some of them may even give you a fright.

Don't worry too much about the formation
It's all in your mind, it's the imagination.

Nicholas Benton (10)
Herne Junior School

OFF TO SCHOOL

Peacefully a child strode to school.
Lonely in the snow
Heavily it came down on her
Dangerously the icy road stretched out before her
Steadily she made her way along the road
Friendly was the cat on the corner
Noisily it miaowed beside her
Lovingly she bent and stroked it
Musically her mobile phone rang
Angrily her mother spoke,
'You have forgotten your books!'

Lisa Gutsell (10)
Herne Junior School

WINTER

Softly the snow fell like a feather.
Loudly the children played in the snow.
Slowly the water turned into ice.
Quickly the families sledged down the slope, like a bicycle going
    down a hill.
Busily the children built a snowman.
Gently the snowflakes fell on their coats, like dust falling to the ground.
Smoothly the children slid on the ice like a pond skater.
Gradually icicles began to grow on the houses.
Noisily the cars drove through the slush.
Hurriedly the children ran inside to get warm.

Victoria White (10)
Herne Junior School

MR NASH

Mr Nash has no cash
His cupboards and wallet lay bare
To get to work he had a mad dash
For the bus, but alas he had not the fare
Off he was thrown
With a grumble and a moan
And the people waving goodbye
So he walked to work with a sigh!

Samantha Crunden (10)
Herne Junior School

RAINDROPS

Raindrops falling through the trees
Like big tears rolling down your cheeks
Splashing on the concrete
Like the sound of horses hooves
Touching frozen ground.
Pitter, patter
The rain goes on,
Touching the leaves of roses red
And dripping to the squelchy earth.
Rushing through the hills and vales
Creating streams and lakes
Across the valleys deep.

Scarlet Sherriff (10)
Iford & Kingston Primary School

MY MUM

My mum is so sweet and oh so tender
She's so cute, but also a big spender.

My mum cares for me when I'm hurt
When I've been rolling in the dirt.

My mum is to cuddle, my mum is to kiss
My mum is to huddle up to and my mum is to miss.

I like my mum lots and lots
And she likes me, 'cos I make pots (and pineapples.)

I hope that my mum will live forever
And never die. Never, never.

Now it's time to say goodbye
I can't believe I've finished, and it's still not July.

I've written this lots and lots of times
And now I've finished – *it rhymes!*

Lucy Harrison (7)
Iford & Kingston Primary School

CLOUDS

Grey and white, soft and fluffy,
Different shapes light and puffy.

Thin and fat, clear and misty,
Wandering slowly, steady and frisky.

Laura Jeffreys (10)
Iford & Kingston Primary School

SOCKS

I'm in an unsatisfactory sock situation,
I'm running round the house in complete frustration.
There's one sock on my bed, one on the floor and
One hiding round the house behind a certain door.

One pink, one blue, now they are a pair,
So when I go to the shops people stop and stare.

They always make the same joke, it falls rather flat,
'Have you got another pair just like that?'

Rose Watts (10)
Iford & Kingston Primary School

TWINKLE TWINKLE LITTLE CAT

Twinkle twinkle little cat,
How I wonder why you're fat .
Sitting on the kitchen floor,
Going through the bedroom door.
Twinkle twinkle little cat,
How I wonder why you're fat.

Alice Bennington (8)
Iford & Kingston Primary School

THE LION

The lion, king of the jungle,
Hanging around in its pride,
Stalking in the long, spiky
Grass on its prey, the scared antelope.
No one would stand in the way
Of a lion.

Sam Webster (10)
Little Common School

OLD SCHOOL

Dusty, dirty, misty, murky.
Boxed, boarded. Shuttered and smashed.
Doors unhung, rusty and unsprung,
Glass and slates, shattered and jagged.
Floor boarding splintered, uneven and cracked,
Walls crumbling and leaning but still.
School grounds desolate and unknown,
Wild bushes and trees are all overgrown.
Empty are the classrooms with cobwebs and grime,
So are the desks all weathered with time.
Children's voices have withered away,
No more do they run, or sing or play.
The blackboard is crusty with old layers of chalk,
Dinner hall empty, nothing left but a fork.
Apparatus corroded, busted and bent,
But the wallbars remain with not even a dent!

Amy Skippings (9)
Little Common School

SUMMER DAYS

The summer is very warm and hot,
A suntan is what I've sometimes got;
The time to sit down and relax,
But you have to keep paying the tax.
Building castles on the sand.
While at the Del-a-War there's a playing band.
People in their colourful boats,
No one in their winter coats!

Louise Mulligan (10)
Little Common School

SUMMER DAYS

Summer is warm and hot,
A suntan is what I've sometimes got.
Finding cockle shells in the sand,
And catching beach balls in my hand.
Seeing animals jumping up high,
And seeing the sunset could make me cry.
When it gets darker I go fishing on the rocks,
And my mum and dad go walking to the docks.
When the sun sets and we go home,
I go and buy my last ice cream cone.
When I get home I go to bed,
Dreaming of summer days in my head.

Emily Taylor (9)
Little Common School

THE GALLOPING HORSE

He gallops along through the fields,
While watching the daisies grow,
He runs so far and long away
Through the trees he gallops
Suddenly he finds himself lost.
He looks around and up and down
He calls a big long neigh
But no one hears.
He tries again and again and again
But still no one cares
The galloping horse lies down
Forever and is never seen again.

Abbi Redman (10)
Little Common School

DOLPHINS

Gliding through the clear waters
A glee to watch
Leaping from the depths
The perfect picture
Smile of cheek lasts forever.

Whines and clicks with the flow
Your noises are happiness
Diving, gliding, flipping and grinning
You flip out of the waters
Let us watch with gaping interest.

You are the sleekest, greyest blue
Silver shines your back
Your body slips through water
Like a swallow
Through thin air.

Anna Walter (9)
Little Common School

IF I WAS A SMALL PERSON

If I was a small person I might get squished,
If I was a small person I could be a borrower.
If I was a small person I could hide and no one would find me.
If I was a small person a flower would be a tree,
If I was a small person an acorn would be a rock.
If I was a small person I could steal lots of sweets.
If I was a small person a face would be a giant,
If I was a small person a leaf would be my home.

Lauren Plimmer (9)
Little Common School

THE SEA

The deeper you go the darker it gets,
Fish get caught in the fishermen's nets,
Winds are all strong,
Waves are all high,
Sailors can't wait to get home in the dry.

The higher the waves, the stronger the sea,
It amazes everyone, even me,
Splishing and splashing the children play,
The sea is beautiful, people say.

The sand glistens like a band of gold,
Runny and soft, sharp to hold,
People like to fish, swim and play in the sea,
Others sit and relax, just like me!

Vicky Cooper (10)
Little Common School

CHRISTMAS EVE

Christmas Eve brings snow that night.
Christmas Eve brings magic for the sight.

Christmas Eve brings icicles long.
Christmas Eve brings the angels' song.

Christmas Eve brings stocking presents small.
Christmas Eve brings a Christmas tree tall.

Christmas Eve brings snow that night.
Christmas Eve brings magic for the sight.

Cara Gooch (10)
Little Common School

THE SOLAR SYSTEM

Go on a voyage through time and history,
See the amazing planets and stars.
Looking, searching for life.
Whiz past the tiny red tomato, Mars,
Rainbow Saturn and its icing rings,
Loop the loop around fiery, mystical Jupiter,
And sink into calmness and peace on Neptune.
Go on holiday to Mercury, but take a lot of sun-cream!
Spin round Uranus and its crystal ball.
Swoop through Venus and its sparkling colours.
Travel to Pluto and discover ancient life forms.
And last, but not least,
The moon and its deep, dangerous craters.

All of these things are a child's dream.

Alice Scotcher (10)
Little Common School

THE LOVE ON THE SEASHORE

The sea glides onto the sand
With a soft whispering sound
Saying 'Love'.

I listen to the seagulls say 'Love',
The people on the pier saying 'Love'.
I open a pearl and it echoes 'Love'.
I will scribe my love into the sand
And it will stain it there forever.

I cannot think of something to explain your love,
It is so powerful.

Jamie Leonard (10)
Little Common School

DOWN IN THE PARK

Down in the park,
I met a boy called Fred,
He said 'I can't play now,
I'm going home to bed.'

Down in the park,
I met a girl called Sue,
She said 'I can't play now,
I need to find a loo.'

Down in the park,
I met a boy called Pat,
He said 'I can't play now,
I'm looking for my cat.'

Down in the park,
I met a girl called Jane,
She said 'I can't play now
I've got a little pain.'

Down in the park,
I met a boy called Frank,
He said 'I can't play now,
I'm going to the bank.'

Down in the park
I met a girl called Rae,
She said 'I can play now
Because I'm here to stay.'

Lauren Black (10)
Little Common School

I AM THE SEA

I am the sea
I draw you under with my calm blue eyes,
Before lashing out with tide-like fingers,
Reaching out to seal your fate.

I am the sea
Chasing the stones high on the beach,
Run away as they chatter and laugh,
Returning again and again.

I am the sea
I rant and rave, then hug you softly
Wrapping you with my whispering words,
Soothing you with my soft, silky, enticing way.

I am the sea!

Tana Isted (11)
Little Common School

SEA

The beautiful sea glistened under the sunlight.
Its white fingers reached out to grab my legs,
The waves called my name as they pulled me towards them.

The twinkling surface raced like horses,
Jumping to and fro,
Days go by and it never disappears, never has and never will.

As the sun sets, the waves die down,
And settle down to sleep,
I say to myself why is it there, why *is* it there?

Shanna Jeans (10)
Little Common School

THE SEA

Wind whips wildly
Awakening the tossing and turning sea
From her deep ocean dream.

Like a magician, the wind turns her sleep to anger.
She swells with rage
And lashes out with her white fingers.

Her calm, smooth, blue-green waves
Turn grey and rough and worrying
As fishermen turn in to shore.

Soon the wind has had its fun.
The sea goes warm and soft,
Exhausted by her day, she lies still and silent.

She gently stirs as happy fishermen throw out their nets.
She is back in her element,
Effacing footprints and melting sandcastles.

Rebecca Barrie (11)
Little Common School

RUGBY

Rugby's what I love
Rugby's what I like
Rugby's what I do
Rugby's fun to play.
Rugby is exciting
Rugby is great fun
And rugby's what I've done
When I was very young!

Elizabeth Francis (9)
Little Common School

DAYS

On windy days
I am rough and bashing.
On calm days
I am mute and gentle.

On sunny days
I am cool and refreshing.
On cold days
I am foaming and warm.

On long days
I am soft and relaxing.
On short days
I am strong and determined.

On busy days
I am friendly and safe.
On lonely days
I am peaceful and still.

Lucy Killick (11)
Little Common School

SUMMER DAYS

The summer is warm and very hot,
A suntan is what I've sometimes got.
The water is cool and like a home
Playing with rocks, sticks and stones.
Eating salad and drinking,
Playing in the sand, sinking.
Going home and having fun,
Having fish and chips, yum yum!

Jasmin Luck (9)
Little Common School

THE SEA AT NIGHT

Like a giant's breath,
Inhaling and exhaling slowly,
The inky blackness of the sea,
Reflexes the moon in its depths.

The white foam of the crashing waves,
Moves closer to the shore,
Crabs scuttle across the sands,
Out of the sea path.

Bobbing yellow lights are the only sights,
Of the fishermen's boats,
Catching tomorrow's supper,
For the people to buy.

Alex Vincent (10)
Little Common School

CHRISTMAS POEM

In the winter there's fun and joy
For every girl and every boy.
The bells are ringing,
The carollers are singing.
Have a happy new year.

The presents are passing,
The lords are dancing.
We kiss under mistletoe,
Father Christmas says 'Ho, ho, ho!'
Have a happy new year.

Rae Gill (10)
Little Common School

SEA

I am rough in the wind,
I am calm in the sun,
I am dangerous,
I am strong.

I have foamy white fingers,
My horses run,
I spit and dribble,
I trap you in my arms.

I am everywhere,
I hold the world,
I will always be here,
From now till forever.
I am the sea.

Jessie Francis (11)
Little Common School

THE HIGHWAY MAN

The Highway Man.
A thief to the bone.
Sleek, quick, hasty.
Like a shadow following your every move.
As quick and as sudden as death.
It makes me feel petrified
Like a fox being chased by hounds.
The Highway Man
As swift as a cat in the shadows.

Fern Kearley (10)
Meeching Valley Primary School

FROM A TWENTY FIRST CENTURY WINDOW

Heavier than birds, heavier than stones
But not as nice as ice cream cones
A lightning bolt struck! As if it was a beam
We were drifting along like twigs in a stream
I see soaking cats
And drying mats
I see people running in their flats
I see people screaming 'Rats!'
Earlier I saw cottages, mansions and a tower
While I was gazing, I ate a sweet, it was so sour
My life is the best
So please be a 21st century guest.

Chris McPherson (10)
Meeching Valley Primary School

SPEEDBOAT

Faster than fishes, faster than trains,
Beaches and people, bridges and planes,
And speeding along like sharks in a race
All through the water the game is at pace
All the sights of the beach and the harbour
Are gathered together in my camera shutter.

Waves splash by and children cry
All together now watch them fly
Flying along in a speedy way
Watching the mast lean at a sway
And I see water and they see land
Playing together on the sand!

Chloe Ware (10)
Meeching Valley Primary School

MONORAIL

Quicker than aeroplanes, quicker than sharks
Into the tunnels and under the arks
Zooming along like a horse on a track
Upwards and downwards, forwards and back
Flowing along in America's land
Better than running through the beach in the sand
There are some people screaming on a ride
And there's someone running over the riverside
There is Disney Land under our feet
Listening to the rhythm of the monorail's beat.

Charlotte Browlett (11)
Meeching Valley Primary School

THE ZOO

In the zoo the monkeys chatter,
hissing snakes silently slither,
parrots squawking, people talking,
the long licking tongue of the lizard,
elephants trumpeting noisy and loud,
all animals getting watched by a big, big crowd.

Katie Gibbs (11)
Meeching Valley Primary School

NIGHT

Night. The moon glistens,
Silence is everywhere,
Only the breeze moves.

Bats rustle the trees,
Thunder clashes in the sky,
Cats watching their prey.

Laura Farley (11)
Meeching Valley Primary School

THE TRAINS

The train chugs along the track,
fast, noisy, long
like an elephant herd,
like a lightning bolt across
the countryside.
It makes me feel glad,
like being at a football match.
The train
reminds us of the Victorian inventions.

Darren Farrant (11)
Meeching Valley Primary School

MOTORBIKE

Quicker than cheetahs, quicker than birds,
Flying along like a rhino in a herd.
People flying past, as I'm really going fast.
If only there was something to make this one day last.
Petrol stations fly along,
Speeding past the petrol pong.
I can't believe I'm riding this monster machine.

Callum Moore (11)
Meeching Valley Primary School

FREE FALL

Free falling out of a plane
Going dizzy, I think I'm insane
A cloud rushing past like a cotton wool ball
I fall, fall, fall and fall.
Scenes of fields, with horses grazing
Farmers ploughing, it's quite amazing!
All of a sudden, I pull the cord
Suddenly the clear air roared.

I am down alone on the ground
Seeing cattle all around
Folding my parachute, enough fun for one day
Parachute packet, walking away
Looking up, the plane overhead
Imagining Spitfires and pilots dead
This is the life I will chose for me
Flying over land and sea!

Aaron Tubb (11)
Meeching Valley Primary School

THE THIEF

The thief
Creeps around at night
Fast, invisible, crafty
As cunning as a fox.
Like a shadow in the fog.
I feel scared that it could be my turn next
It makes me feel a teacher is looking over my shoulder.
The thief
Makes me feel that my safety is the most important thing.

Lauren Seymour-Steed (10)
Meeching Valley Primary School

FROM A 21ST CENTURY WINDOW

Speeding along underground in the dark,
Tracks glowing, sparks flowing.
Speeding through the tunnel,
It's getting pretty dark,
Like diving into a body
Of a monstrous black shark.

By and by, we come to a stop,
Leaves on the line, it's one o'clock.
I hurry off the electric train,
Only to be late for work again!

Hollie Groucutt (10)
Meeching Valley Primary School

SLEEPING LIKE AN ANIMAL

I'm lying in a bamboo tree.
Looking down at the floor, ssh!
It's a Burmese python looking at me,
Then it slithered through the autumn leaves.
'Roar' said the preying mantis.
Ahh! I jumped down and started running
I stopped and found that I was in a bush.
A head popped out, miaow!
Phew, it's only a cat, I wonder what type?
Ahh! It's a lion.
Gulp!
Gone.

Steven Franks (9)
Ninfield C of E School

SPACE VOYAGE

I'm captain of my spaceship,
Which goes so very fast,
Soaring through the galaxy,
With stars shooting past.

Asteroids, comets and moons,
Planets even shaped like spoons!
I've seen them all!
Even giant cocoons!

Giant Black Holes,
And little moles,
All the way to Earth,
It gets right to the soul!

Now it's time to end this poem,
But when you're deep in love,
Don't forget me and the stars above!

Tony Borrell (10)
Ninfield C of E School

STARS

Stars, stars, shooting stars,
Stars above and stars below,
Shooting up through the sky
Most of them go whistling by.

They want to eat a piece of the moon,
But none of it will fit on a spoon.
The stars will go to sleep,
Goodbye stars, I'll see you soon.

Nicholas Mayes (10)
Ninfield C of E School

My Little Friends

There's Ted my bear that sits on my bed,
He has a rather fluffy head.
Then there's Ben, he's a little baby hen,
His favourite number is ten.
There's ducky as well,
Who I tuck in my bed.
And I say 'Night, night my little friend.'
I also have lots, lots more,
So I don't think I'll ever get bored.
I have Hippie the hedgehog and
Freddy the frog and a lovely cat called Mog!

Marisa Reid (9)
Ninfield C of E School

In The Forest

Can you hear the people camping?
Can you hear the water splashing
Against the rocks?

Can you hear the wind rushing?
Can you hear wild horses galloping
In the meadows?

Can you hear the trees rustling?
Can you hear the foxes shuffling
In the long grass?

Mark Sayer (10)
Ninfield C of E School

DOLPHINS

Dolphins, dolphins,
Swim around
Watch the dolphins leap and bound.

Dolphins, dolphins,
As fun as can be
They are clever just like me!

Dolphins, dolphins,
Communicate really loud
Dolphins should be very proud.

Dolphins, dolphins,
Bluey grey
I wonder what they do all day?

Dolphins, dolphins,
Eat lots of fish
But they don't eat them in a dish.

Dolphins, dolphins,
Flip their fins
They don't put their rubbish in bins.

Charlotte Cannon (9)
Ninfield C of E School

BOOKS

I like books,
Some are funny,
Some are sad,
Some are gripping,
Some are mad!

I like authors,
J K Rowling,
Gillian Cross,
Jacqueline Wilson,
Without them I'd be at a loss.

Elena Matthews (10)
Ninfield C of E School

WE'RE ON OUR WAY TO FORREST HILL

Leeds are playing at home,
Last time we played, we played at Rome,
At Rome we won 3-0,
Now we're going to Forrest Hill.

We have joy, we have fun,
We have Arsenal on the run,
But the fun didn't last,
Because Bergkamp was too fast.

Finally we got there.
We saw people with fake hair,
In the end we won 5-1.
We have Arsenal on the run.

We have joy, we have fun,
We have Arsenal on the run.
But the fun didn't last,
Because Bergkamp was too fast.

Danny Austin (11)
Ninfield C of E School

FANCY THAT

Fancy that, fancy that,
A furry monster down the street.

Fancy that, fancy that,
The pavement's singing high and sweet.

Fancy that, fancy that,
A tiger's flying a big green kite.

Fancy that, fancy that,
An aerial took off with wings so white.

Fancy that, fancy that,
All this I saw while going to school.

Fancy that, fancy that,
I never quite got over it all.

Leah Allen (11)
Ninfield C of E School

FLAT THE CAT

I was driving down the road one day.
I heard a little spat!
I wonder what it was?
Then I thought it was my cat!
I jumped into the back seat,
Did not know what to do!
I saw my cat,
It didn't go splat.
But my sister was lying there too!

Poppy Anderson (11)
Ninfield C of E School

DOWN THE MOTORWAY

On the M25,
Dad's car came alive.
Stuttering, starting,
Trundling and darting.

We're nearly all out of unleaded,
It's what we really dreaded.
We could be crushed,
We could be mushed.

We jumped out of the car,
It went off with a zoom.
I'm glad we were out of it,
It blew up with a boom!

James Freeman (10)
Ninfield C of E School

WRESTLING

WWF, better than WCW and all the rest.
Rock is simply the best.
Evil comes from the Undertaker.
Stone Cold is a trouble maker.
Tazz needs to keep his cool.
Lita, for a woman, is too tall.
Intelligence, integrity, intensity are what you need.
New wrestlers I hope will do a good deed.
Good Will Ambassador William Regal
Should be quiet for once.

Peter Davies (10)
Ninfield C of E School

MY OLD FRIEND ROCKER-ROO

My old friend Rocker-Roo,
Didn't know what to do,
He sat watching football being bored,
Until Leeds United almost scored.

Rocker-Roo supported Leeds you know,
He also likes The Simpsons, Doh!
One day he went to see Leeds play,
He got a forged ticket so he didn't have to pay.

Rocker-Roo wasn't bored anymore,
He went to his bedroom and opened the drawer,
He found the most unusual thing he could ever imagine,
It was Rocker-Roo in a picture so thin.

Nick Coughlan (11)
Ninfield C of E School

SCHOOL!

Wake up! Stop messing about,
Now calm down class or I'll shout!
Jamie please get me a pencil,
Luke, why do you have a hen?
Oh sorry Miss, I forgot my pen.

Class line up,
Veairl, please don't touch the pup.
Playing on the field, playing ball,
Miss, Miss I need to go to the hall.

Joeley Elphick (10)
Ninfield C of E School

A BAD JOURNEY

The roaring sea crashed against the rocks,
The seaweed held on for dear life at the bottom of the ocean,
Limpets closed their shells,
Sea worms were tied in knots.
Animals were spun around like lotion in a bottle,
The ship rose across the sea like bells ringing.
Men were moaning,
Supplies were running out,
Lives were disappearing like dust,
The ship was going out of control.
It was a bad journey,
It took weeks, days
But we made it.

Laura Chaplin (10)
Park Mead C P School

FIREWORKS

Fireworks, fireworks shooting high,
Going higher as they fly.
Multi-coloured flowers in the sky.
Bangs and crackles everywhere.
Ricocheting across the night air.
Brightness lingers like a flare.
The magic makes you stop and stare.

Jade Chittenden (10)
Park Mead C P School

A VOYAGE

A voyage that goes from place to place,
A voyage to see the human race.
A voyage that takes me far away,
A voyage that takes night and day.
A voyage on the ocean wave,
A voyage to make me really brave.
A voyage to make me surf and save,
A voyage to meet a brand new world
Of dolphins, fish and whales too –
And now my journey is at its end,
After seeing the creatures jump and bend.

Eleanor Risbridger (8)
Park Mead C P School

A VOYAGE THROUGH TIME

Time flies when you're in my magic machine,
A voyage through time,
A voyage through time.

Outside in the mist, the mast with a flag is flapping, flapping.

A shooting star in the sky is flying, flying,
And then all is silent
We reach our final destination, destination.

Emily Dann (10)
Park Mead C P School

COCKROACH WRITES A LOVE POEM TO HIS WIFE

My black, slimy wife,
With a vicious, shiny, sharp tail,
You're always grumpy to make me happy,
You scare off people to make me proud,
You riffle all night in the rubbish,
You're so brave when the cats come.

Cockroach Writes A Love Poem To Her Husband

You scuttle and scamper around,
You scavenge around like I don't know what.
Your horrible hitting is nice in all kinds of ways,
Your serious stinger is your tail,
And is the best thing I like.

Siobhan Zysemil (10)
Peasmash C of E Primary School

SCORPIONS' LOVE SONG

Oh, my stingy, storky stallion,
With your pinchers sharp and bright.
Your sting is as red as a Ferrari,
You almost make me blind.

Your googly eyes are so glamorous,
You make me shiver inside.
Your long tail is bigger than mine,
When you go, you always make me pine.
Your body is slimy and gooey.

Ricky Piggott (10)
Peasmash C of E Primary School

THE WOLF'S POEM

Monday's child is good to roast,
Tuesday's child is good to toast,
Wednesday's child is so good, moist and runny,
Thursday's child is really funny,
Friday's child is best in honey.
Saturday's child is delicious in honey.
The child that is born on the Sabbath day is delicious anyway.

Tyler Watson (11)
Peasmash C of E Primary School

AUTUMN

The icy breeze blows past the trees,
Swirling the brown leaves around,
Chestnuts hanging on the tree,
Conkers lay on the ground.

Terry Page (10)
Peasmash C of E Primary School

AUTUMN POEM

Harvest is fun
Autumn leaves on the ground
Red leaves on the ground
Vines going brown
Scary Hallowe'en is on the way.
Summer has gone and autumn is here,
Too cold to play.

Samantha Richards (9)
Peasmash C of E Primary School

PLATYPUS POEM

Mr Platypus:

Oh my webbed, wonderful wife,
How do you get in such strife?
With your fur coloured coat.
I will kill a stoat to keep your vote.
With my beaver tail I would whack a snail,
To keep the slime off you.

Mrs Platypus:

Oh my smoochy soft husband,
With your goggly eyes you really give me a surprise.
With your chubby belly, you're not so smelly in the daytime,
But in the night you give me a fright.

Danny Walton (9)
Peasmash C of E Primary School

SUDDENLY

Suddenly the waves crashed to the shore.
Suddenly the crab smashed his claw.

Suddenly the plane crashed.
Suddenly the rain splashed.

Suddenly the computer disappeared.
Suddenly the magician reappeared.

Suddenly the magnets clung together.
Suddenly we were lost for ever and ever.

Chrissie Wall (9)
Peasmash C of E Primary School

HORNY DEVIL WRITES A LOVE POEM TO HIS WIFE

Oh my beautiful stressed wife
Who takes away my life,
You are so wobbly
My woolly fat wife
You are always pregnant
You bite my head off
You love to sleep in the hay.

Mrs Ewe Writes A Love Poem To Her Husband

Oh my beautiful horny devil,
You're so lovely to cuddle
My hubby is so chubby
You have never had mates
You are strong and sometimes a wimp
My funny, white hubby
You are so aggressive.

Felicity Barnes (11)
Peasmash C of E Primary School

THE SNOW ROBIN

Look at the little robin,
Twittering in a tree.

There goes the little robin,
Flying out to sea.

He passes the baker's shop,
And he stops for a bun,
Then he goes on his way,
To have a bit of fun.

Philippa Dunn (9)
Peasmash C of E Primary School

THE BEAR AND THE ECHO

The monstrous bear with all his might,
Gave a roar in the middle of the night.
The roar came back and to his fright,
He heard another roar bold and bright.

'Show yourself, you coward, I know you're near!'
in a little bit of fear.
Then to his surprise he could hear,
The bear replying 'near, near, near.'

'Come out, come out, you know I'm the best.
How dare you disturb my rest?'
But the other bear seemed to protest,
'I'm the best, I'm the best.'

Frightened by every sound he heard,
He called upon the wise bird.
She said 'every time the voice you hear,
Is simply the voice of your own fear.'

Katie Thomas (10)
Peasmash C of E Primary School

SNOW

People are building snowmen,
As the snow starts to fall.
A snowdrop glitters into the sky,
It glitters away into the darkness.
Falling on rooftops,
Falling off rooftops onto the ground.
Deeper and deeper and turns into water.

Leoni Ennis (10)
Peasmash C of E Primary School

PIGLET WRITES A LOVE POEM TO HIS WIFE

My porkful, fat wife.
Every time I see you my tail goes up in curls.
I can't stop looking at your wibbly, wobbly walk.
You snorty, chubby babe.
With your big beautiful body.
You make me feel so good. Oink!

Piglet Writes A Love Poem To Her Husband

My fat, muddy partner.
Every time I see you I give a great big squeak!
You are my squeaky, chubby toy.
You are my only pork chops.
I don't know what I would do without you.
You make me feel so fat.

Luke Sothcott (10)
Peasmash C of E Primary School

SNOW-WOLF

So cold in the wolf's cave of snow,
Across the floor turns white.
The cubs turn to ice in the freezing cold.
When the wolf finds food, he kills it in a bite.
When kids play snowballs by the cave
He frightens them off with his loudest roar.
When hunters come to shoot him down
He runs off faster than a wild boar.

Ben Baker (10)
Peasmash C of E Primary School

CHEETAH WRITES A LOVE POEM TO HIS WIFE

Oh, my black spotted wife
Sleek, yellow in my life
Your juicy, luscious lips
Your wet nose shining in the summer sun
Your wonderful wagging tail.

Cheetah Writes A Love Poem To Her Husband

Oh, my chilly cheetah
With your chattering lips
Faster than a snail
Your lovely magnificent tail
Oh, my lovey-dovey slim cheetah
Scaring things away with your sharp teeth.

Kirsty Juden (9)
Peasmash C of E Primary School

FISHY LOVE

To my earnest-eyed escort,
When your luminous, luscious lips come near me I blush.
Your blossoming bubbles are pretty and neat,
Your dainty dorsal fin and tender tail waves gently through the water.
I love your slimy scales, they feel so smooth.
I like it when our harmonious heads rub together.

To my hunky-headed hubby,
Your threatening tail and boisterous bubbles protect me.
I love the way your charming colour changes,
Your flapping fins are handsome.
I really, really love you,
Even when you're grumpy.

Jade Bull (10)
Peasmash C of E Primary School

WORM'S LOVE POEM TO HIS WIFE

Oh my beautiful soft, slimy wife.
You will be with me all your life.
You're so long and thin.
That's why you send me in a spin.
As you wiggle through the mud, your soft pink skin gets all muddy.
Even though you get all muddy you will always be the best.

The Worm's Love Poem To Her Husband

Oh my handsome hubby-dubby, always in a hurry.
Whenever you come home for lunch you always cook a curry.
When you stretch your pink wrinkled skin.
You always know it makes my heart pound.

Danielle Watts (10)
Peasmash C of E Primary School

SLUG WRITES A LOVE POEM TO HIS WIFE

My slimy, slithering, scatty thing,
Wriggling wildly around,
My wrinkly-skinned baby,
You're not making much sound,
You are my bubbly, slimy babe,
But you never shave.

Slug Writes A Love Poem To Her Husband

My delicious, dirty hubby,
Who is very lovey-dovey,
My lovely, luscious hubby, slimy and similar to me,
My drunken, slimy thing,
Squelching home from the bin.

Donna-Marie Maplesden (10)
Peasmash C of E Primary School

MR SNAIL AND MRS SNAIL'S LOVE POEM

Mr Snail's Love Poem:

Oh my lovey-dovey, slimy mate.
Oh how I love your squidgy body.
The way you move all slow and sorry.
I love you when you get drunk as a skunk every night.
Your lovely swirly shell makes you handsome.
I think your slithery, sexy body attracts every other snail.

Mrs Snail's Love Poem:

Oh how glamorous your body shines.
People say I'm lucky.
Your pointy long eyes make you beautiful and I adore you.
But I think you're fat and chunky.
Your trail tells me where you are.
I think we should marry, that would be good.

Jessica Beale (10)
Peasmash C of E Primary School

SNOWY WONDERLAND

Gentle snowflakes fall to the ground.
Watch them fall.
See all the snow we discovered.
Watch the children make a snowball.
The adults build an igloo.
All the children play.
Later they crowd around the fire.
They all know it's the end of the day.

William Henry Nye (9)
Peasmash C of E Primary School

RUNNING LOVERS

Cheetah write a love poem to his wife:

Oh my swift running wife,
You are quicker than my life lane.
When I miss my prey, I just want to cuddle you.
You catch the thing that I want.
A zebra I will kill for you.
Oh I miss you when you hunt.

Cheetah writes a love poem to her husband:

Oh my deadly murderer, how I admire you.
I love your razor claws and teeth.
You are my crazy companion.
I love your blotty back.
You could be the best engine.
I adore your wet nose, it is the best.

Thomas Martin (10)
Peasmash C of E Primary School

DOUGHNUTS

Doughnuts come in different flavours,
Bubble gum sprinkles and ice cream swirls.
Round ones, fat ones and some that curl.
One bite, two bites, three bites, *gone!*

Callum Laverton (10)
Peasmash C of E Primary School

LOVE POEM TO HIS WIFE

Oh my skinniest wife
So tiny and black
You've got the smallest wings
You are the furriest ever.
You are so light
You are the slimiest ever
We are the nastiest in the world.

Love Poem To Her Husband

Oh my fattest husband
You're the fattest husband I have ever had
You are the biggest husband in the family
You have got the smallest wings.

Can you guess what we are?
We are flies.

Matthew Saunders (10)
Peasmash C of E Primary School

AUTUMN POEM

Sunny yellows glistening in the sun.
Golden fields being ploughed for harvest.
Apples ready for eating.
Leaves cracking under my feet.
Yellowing hedges, shining in the golden sun.

Robbie Fritchley (11)
Peasmash C of E Primary School

CARP WRITES TO HIS WIFE

Oh my fat cuddly wife,
I loved you all my life.
I love your eyes,
As big as pies.
How brave you are when you see a rod,
The fishermen are very odd.
You are my curious companion.

Carp Writes To Her Husband

Oh my fatter, cuddly husband,
I love you so much.
How big and brave you are,
We have travelled so far.
You're a very hard fighter,
And a very good frightener.
You are a cuddly companion.

Philip Greenough (11)
Peasmash C of E Primary School

WHEN TWILIGHT COMES

When twilight comes the sun is tucked
Away under the horizon
Leaving a fraction of light for us to see.

When twilight comes shadows highlight
The ground and badgers come out from
Under a tree.

When twilight comes a barn owl glides
Over a field as it pinpoints a mouse
Scurrying by.

When twilight ends it is as black as night
But not as light as twilight's sky.

Kalon Richfield (10)
Rodmell C of E School

NO EXCUSES PLEASE!

I'm sick
I'm ill
I've got pimples on my tum
And my homework's not done!
Who cares, not me for one!

My teacher's very sad!
'Cause I'm very bad
She had a bright red face
I was in disgrace
My homework was not done!

Head Teacher here I come
My homework was not done
She caught me chewing gum
Detention here I come!

I really was ill
Honest!

Ben Taylor (10)
Rodmell C of E School

THE NEW ARRIVALS

It is still
It is quiet
It is peaceful in the shed.
They arrive
All at once
With straw for their bed!
They are soft
They are warm
They have skin that's marshmallow pink.
They cannot eat
They squeak to talk
There is lots of warm milk to drink!
They soundly sleep
They are naughty at times
They have tails like wound up springs!
Mum is kind
Mum is proud
She treats them all like kings!

What are they?
Piglets of course!

Lauren Taylor (10)
Rodmell C of E School

NIGHT HAIKU

Night washes away
The daylight sky and brings out
Creatures in the night.

Laura Reed (10)
Rodmell C of E School

SNOW FROLICS

It's a cold dark night
Thousands of glittery stars light
Up the sky.
The flakes fall
Children love to play
In the crisp white snow!

There is a snowball fight
The balls are round and sparkling bright
The boys win that night!

A snowman is built
He's wearing a kilt
A true Scot!

Out comes the sun
Away goes the fun
Pools of water are found
Is it the melted snow?
Or our tears of disappointment?

Nicholas Taylor (10)
Rodmell C of E School

WIND

It blows like a hurricane.
Washing its wings.
Floats like a butterfly
High in the sky.

Sheree Donaldson (10)
Rodmell C of E School

THE JOURNEY THAT TOOK FOREVER

The journey that took forever,
Started in my back street.
The journey that took forever,
Included snow, hail and sleet.

The journey that took forever,
Always began in day,
The journey that took forever,
Always took years away.

The journey that took forever,
Ended in the eve.
The journey that took forever,
Made me want to leave.

The journey that took forever,
Was a waste of time.
The journey that took forever,
Made the night bells chime.

The journey that took forever,
Seemed to take all day.
The journey that took forever,
Ended happy in a way.

The journey that took forever,
Was a boring night.
The journey that took forever,
Finished in a fright.

The journey that took forever,
Made me take the pain.
The journey that took forever,
Oh no! Not again.

Alex Pettitt (11)
Rodmell C of E School

THE WITCH'S CAT

Every day I walk to my village school,
I hear the patter of paws, in the corner of my eye I see
A shadow which makes me shudder,
Which I call . . .
The witch's cat.

Its whiskers curl,
I thought I almost caught a slow, sly smile spread across
Its dark face.
Suddenly, I did a twirl . . .
Was it here? The witch's cat?

Then at last, the bell, it goes,
A moving cloud blocks the sun, but there is still a
Flash of green, bright, staring eyes,
Was it? Who knows?
Was it? The eyes of . . . The witch's cat?

Why won't he just go away?
I had an argument with my friend today,
Now she is a frog!

You can always rely on Miss Spellman's cat,
The witch's cat.

Anastasia Bell (10)
Rodmell C of E School

THE WIND

Wind is sometimes very powerful
Wind can blow down loads of buildings
Wind moves the washing backwards and forwards
Wind, you can't see it but you can feel it.
The wind.

Kerry Barrett (10)
Rodmell C of E School

In the Woods

Crackling in the leaves
The moonlight shines
On the trees,
When people are walking in the breeze.

Owls looking in the big blue sky
Birds whistling all the time, birds' feathers
Flying by as the breeze passes by.

The wind is twisting all around,
The branches are crackling to the ground.
Rabbits are running to their warren,
To escape the whirling wind that
Is rushing past.

Lisa James (9)
Rodmell C of E School

Hallowe'en

Pumpkin, bumpkin
Tucked up tight.
Saw a witch in the night.
Flying high she hopes to die,
She's going to the graveyard
To go to bed with all her scary
Thoughts in her head.

She's going through the mist,
To find her grave.
Ssh! Don't make a peep,
Winnie is trying to sleep.

Oliver Dale (9)
St Leonard's C of E Primary School

MY HAMSTER

My hamster is grey.
She was born in May.

My hamster lives in a cage.
She sometimes gets in a rage.

She is very fat
And she hates the cat.

I have another hamster
She's got a bigger cage.
I feel sorry for my little hamster
She bites her cage and
Tries to get out.
She likes to run about
And roll in her ball
She's my little hamster.

Samantha Pont (10)
St Leonard's C of E Primary School

HUMPTY DUMPTY WENT TO SPACE

Humpty Dumpty went to space
On a supersonic face.
Humpty Dumpty saw Mars
Humpty Dumpty saw Neptune
Humpty Dumpty saw Earth
Humpty Dumpty saw the stars
Humpty Dumpty please come home
And enjoy the Millennium Dome.

Grant Searle (9)
St Leonard's C of E Primary School

MY BEST FRIEND

My best friend's name is Ollie,
I met him in year one.
We have played together since
And had lots of fun.

My best friend is Ollie,
I met him in year one.
When he invites me round his house
We have lots of fun.
And when it's time to go we say
'Just a little longer.'
The answer is always 'No.'
But we know that
We will see each other tomorrow.

My best friend is Ollie,
I met him in year one.
We have played together since
And had lots of fun.

He's the best friend you could have!

Jade Worboys (9)
St Leonard's C of E Primary School

MY PET CAT

My pet cat is like a lion.
King of the jungle,
King of the house.

She's black and brown,
With a bit of grey.
Not ragged like a lion.

She hunts for mice
And scares away foxes.

She jumps and pounces
But purrs when I pet her.
She is the best cat in the world
And I love her.

Sarah Giff (10)
St Leonard's C of E Primary School

MY PET PARROT

My pet parrot squeaks
He is really noisy!

He enjoys bananas
And sunflower seeds.

He hates men and boys
He bites their little fingers.

He is a great parrot
And I think he is cute.

He is green and grey
His eyes are green and black.

And I love him so much
He is the best parrot.

Elena Bryan (10)
St Leonard's C of E Primary School

MY RAT

My rat is big and round although he is a clown.
My rat knows where my room is.
His tail is pink and long,
His eyes are black,
His fur is grey and he has his own house.

When my rat is scared he jumps up in the air then
Runs round and most likely will bite someone.
His house is white with a hole in it and cracks.
But as long as I don't lose him everything is OK.
My mum gave him to someone else.
I was in tears.
I've got over it now.
I miss him so much it seems like a tragedy
I guess I will just have to put up with it.

Ricky Wackett (9)
St Leonard's C of E Primary School

PLANETS

Planets though so far away,
In such magnificence and brilliance.
I'd like to visit them so far way
In the sky.
In a rocket that will fly high.
Land on them and stay to have a little play.
Now shooting home past meteorites.
Now landing back on Earth.
What a magnificent sight.
England's miserable weather actually seems
Quite nice.

Josh Murphy (10)
St Leonard's C of E Primary School

THE PLANETS

The sun is hot
Mars is cold
Saturn has a ring like a king.

The moon is large
Neptune is big
Pluto is small like a ball.

Jupiter is windy
Venus is warm
Mercury is the nearest to the sun.

Earth was made
For you and me
To live happily.

Abbie Entecott (10)
St Leonard's C of E Primary School

PETS!

Cats are soft,
Dogs are mad,
Hamsters are calm and noisy
And that's a variety of pets.

Cats are sweet,
Mice are tiny,
Lizards are long
And that's just a few pets.

Cats are cuddly,
Fish are calm,
Rats are tame,
And that's some more about pets.

Danielle Smith (10)
St Leonard's C of E Primary School

MARY ROSE

The Mary Rose travelled the Seven Seas
To battle the French.

The wind was a strong as iron
The waves as big as a giraffe.

Bang went the French guns.

Down went the Mary Rose

Everyone was screaming
And scrambling to get out.

There went the Mary Rose
Like the soap
At the bottom of the bath.

Joshua Reyniers (10)
St Leonard's C of E Primary School

CATS AND DOGS

Cats scratch
My cat doesn't.

Dogs bark
My dog doesn't.

Cats purr
My cat does.

Dogs wag their tails
My dog does.

Cats like going outside
My cat doesn't.

Dogs jump up
But my dog doesn't.

Connor Bradford (9)
St Leonard's C of E Primary School

WAR HOUSE

We all rush to the air raid shelter,
Dad, Mum and me.

German planes I see.
I hope they're not going to bomb us.

Dad's saying a prayer 'Help us! Help us!'
Mum's squeezing me!

Spitfires I see
Go! Go! Get the Germans!

It's all gone quiet,
The noise has disappeared.
'I think the war's over!' announces Dad
'Let's party!'

Alice Howard (9)
St Leonard's C of E Primary School

I LOVE DOGS

I love dogs, they're cuddly and cute.
They follow me everywhere
'Cos they think I have food.

My dogs are clever
They keep me safe and warm.
I always play ball with them on the lawn
Sometimes night. Sometimes morn.

I take them for a walk day and night.
If they saw another they would never bite.
Dogs are lovely, dogs are the best
And all the rest are alright.

Blake Cornwall (10)
St Leonard's C of E Primary School

MY BEST FRIEND

My best friend is Emma,
Between her and my family it's a dilemma,
She comes to my house to play,
We see each other nearly every day.

My mum and her mum are good friends,
My brother is good friends with her brother,
Her dad and my dad are friends,
Me and Emma are best friends.

We've been best friends since reception,
We've had a few fallouts but we got back together,
I just want her to know that I like her very much,
And I hope we stay good friends forever.

Sarah Burgess (10)
St Leonard's C of E Primary School

WAR WORLD

The war is coming,
All load the guns,
(Our clothes are now like litter)
Come on through the trench,
Clump, clump, bang!

The torture spreads everywhere,
Bullets shoot at my legs,
The trench fills with water,
Bugs and lice in our uniforms!

I hear marching feet,
And screaming bombs blasting,
I hear the propellers spin
From the air force fleet.

Rotting bodies are in the camps,
Moaning bodies in no-man's land,
Longing for their home, on brown grass;
Starving!

I see swelling bodies; I am sweating
In a claustrophobic room,
With little food or water,
I try to get out, there's bullets everywhere!

I'm half dead,
With poppies the only flowers left.

I stare into the long lost soldier's eyes.
Dead faces, but bodies still alive;
Rocks are everywhere,
Flags held high!

Joseph Moffatt (9)
St Mary's RC Primary School

WINTER WONDERLAND

Sledging down the steep white hill,
While Jack Frost nibbles at your nose.
You're in the world of Christmas cards,
People and animals leave their marks,
Until the thaw starts.

I'm sitting next to the still warm fire
Watching the crystals cascade to the ground.
Look and watch them dancing, prancing.
Swirling, twirling, thick and fast.
A carpet of white, tumbling, gradually calmer.

Soft, new snow lies still and thick,
Shimmering on the broad, white field,
Where cattle usually graze.
All the hay is frozen, rock hard.
Then drip, drop. It's all gone.
We'll have to wait for the next Christmas card.

Lauren Clifton (9)
St Mary's RC Primary School

WHITE FALLING CRYSTALS

I woke up and looked outside,
And saw the ice cold snow,
My sister and I jumped with joy,
We played outside all day long,
Until it was time to go.

We went to bed,
And couldn't get to sleep,
I woke up the next morning,
And saw the most beautiful thing.

So we went outside to play on the carpet of snow,
Suddenly all was quiet and calm,
And we built a snowman,
Then went sledging,
And it was like a crystal Christmas dream come true.

Frances Upton (9)
St Mary's RC Primary School

WORLD WAR TWO

Towards the trenches I march,
With such a feeling of dread.
Already I'm longing for home.
I join the others wailing in the mess, the smell.
It starts.
Over the top, gunshots resound.
Mud, exploding mud spatters over me.
Screams of terror surround me.
Men are dying.
So much blood,
So much gore.
Back in the trenches, I slump,
Exhausted, but alive.
Hunger eats me,
But there is little food or water.
With the moaning all around me,
Claustrophobia is setting in.
Next to me people are dying, limbs lost.
I long so much for home.
Now, here I stand with my memories.
Of that place where once rotting bodies lay,
Replaced by fields of poppies, blood red.
I shall never forget.

Miranda Davis (9)
St Mary's RC Primary School

AMBITIONS, AMBITIONS!

When I grow up I want to be a doctor or a nurse,
Or maybe a millionaire with loads of cash in my purse.
I could be an air-hostess, or an author, that would be fab!
Or should I be a scientist, working away in my lab?
Or maybe I could be an actress, star of the show,
I suppose I could be in the army, but that would be tough, I know.
What about a popstar, as good as Madonna, no greater.
Or I could be a world champion roller-skater!
I could be in the Olympics, swimming or riding a bike,
But for now, I'll just be me, a lazy little tyke!

Erin Cardiff (9)
St Mary's RC Primary School

REMEMBRANCE DAY POEM

Many a tear fills the eye,
At thoughts of men who had to die,
For you and me to live in peace.
And be free.
A solemn thought of pain and sorrow,
For those men who died for our tomorrow.

Hannah Woodward (9)
St Mary's RC Primary School

MY SNOW POEM

Snow is falling, snow is settling,
No one's about in this white world.
I'm watching it fall, tumble, swirl, twirl,
Watching it form a carpet of white,
Oh, what a pretty sight.

Crystals are twinkling as the sun comes out,
Icicles are dazzling as bright as stars,
Oh, the snow it feels so soft and thick,
As calm as a beautiful dream.

My cheeks are bright red with coldness,
I think I've got frostbite in my toes,
There's my mum, she's calling me,
So night, night snow.

Krystina Divon (9)
St Mary's RC Primary School

I'M PLAYING IN THE SNOW

It's snowing right now.
So I'm sitting by the raging fire.
The white, swirling and twisting crystals,
Come fluttering down outside.
I put on my hat and coat,
And go out into the winter wonderland.
I'm sledging down a thickly covered hillside.
Trying very hard not to crash.
Snowballs come flying past me.
Hooray! I'm having so much fun.
Now it's time for bed.
What a wonderful day I've had.
So magical, so much fun and so white in the snow.

Tanya Romans (10)
St Mary's RC Primary School

THE WEREWOLF

Every night I hear someone or something howl,
It gives me the spooks.
I cover my ears and slip under the bed cover,
Then, I hope to get some sleep.

Later, I wake up,
I go to investigate.
Guess what,
Two nights ago I found five clues.

The clues were,
A bottle of werewolf dribble,
Two werewolf hairs, a werewolf's skull,
And a werewolf's leg bone.

Yesterday I looked at them very carefully,
And I'm sure what I heard was a werewolf.
Tomorrow I'm going on a werewolf hunt,
Of course, I'm going with my friends.

Today's the day,
It's the day I find the werewolf.
I've brought some bits and pieces,
That we might need on the journey.

It's the next day now,
Guess what we did?
We found the werewolf,
And brought it home,

And now it's our
Pet!

Elizabeth Marshall (9)
St Mary's RC Primary School

THE GIANT

One day I flew to a castle
High above the sky.
Knocking gently on the door,
Gushing sounds came to my ears.
Huge doors opened.
A massive giant picked me up,
His eyes swirling out of his head.
He opened his terrible mouth,
Teeth all cracked and mouldy.
He put me in,
But spat me out.
I tasted funny.
I flew home at tremendous speed
And landed softly in my bed.

Alex Scott (9)
Sacred Heart School

THE MOON

The moon is bright
When in sight
But the sun
Has its own light
I am fond of the moon
Reflecting from the sun
I wish I was an astronaut
I would rule the moon
Forever.

Thomas Neeves (8)
Sacred Heart School

JELLY WOBBLES

Jelly wobbles to and fro
Off the plate it will go.
Up the trees,
Through the meadow
Then back again.
Wobbling jelly comes and goes
Ending up inside . . .
Your tummy!

Joshua Thorneycroft (7)
Sacred Heart School

THE JOURNEY OF A SNAKE

Slowly slithering across the floor.
Looking high and looking low.
Catching his prey with
A bite of his jaw.
Swallowing in one gulp.
Through the leaves.
Quickly he goes.
Returning to his home.

Gabriella Feachem (8)
Sacred Heart School

THE BABY

The baby was in a cradle
Rocking, rocking away.
A tear was running
Down his chubby face.

But Mother came
She picked him up
And with one sniff,
He fell asleep.

Emma Weddell (8)
Sacred Heart School

MY SISTER IS A PAIN

My sister is such a pain
I wish I could hit her with a cane.
She scribbles all over my books.
The teacher says
How dreadful it looks.
I really wish she would go away
And leave me in peace for just a day.
Oh I wish, oh I wish, oh I wish!

Kate Bossie (8)
Sacred Heart School

THE SNAIL

The snail I saw,
Was slimy and sticky,
I picked it up,
It felt as if,
It licked me,
So I put it in the soil,
He hid in his shell.

Stephanie Sohail (8)
Sacred Heart School

ANIMALS

Dogs are fun to play with and they are man's best friend,
Cats are sweet, cuddly, loveable and quiet.
Guinea-pigs are soft, gentle, lovely creatures,
Hamsters are quick, fast, slim and intelligent,
Rabbits are friendly, quick and they love the attention.
Fish have a three second memory and they are very boring.

Emily Brazier (11)
Sacred Heart School

THE LITTLE FISH

The little fish was small and bright
Glowing in the light.
He liked to jump about
And swim in the ocean deep.
He hunts for worms
In the mud
And follows the other fish.

Chloe Silver (9)
Sacred Heart School

HANDS

I love my hands
Like elastic bands.
Like string
They cling
Onto my wrists.
But I have fists
To punch my brother.
I love my hands.

Katie Field (8)
Sacred Heart School

THE CREATURE

I've heard of this creature
It sounds pretty scary,
It rips,
It tears,
It's very mad.
It could be climbing up the stairs,
So run and hide in any place,
In the cupboard,
In the bed.
With this picture
Running through your head,
Close your eyes
Don't take a peek.
Oh! It's just my mum.

Harry Austin (9)
Sacred Heart School

THE DEVIL

The devil, the devil,
He is a terrible thing.
The devil, the devil,
Smiling his wicked grin.
His wings are on fire,
His horns blazing red.
His piercing scream,
Awakening the dead.
I hate him, I hate him.
That devil in red . . .

Caroline Mackrill (9)
Sacred Heart School

BORING DAYS

At home it is so boring
It is like I am about to start snoring,
Nothing is exciting
It is like doing homework and writing.

When it has to rain
It is always the same
Nothing to do, nothing to play
All I do is watch TV all day.

When I sit inside
I want to go on a roller coaster ride.
When I sit inside all day
Nothing to do, nothing to play.
I said to my mum 'what am I to do?'
She said 'I will go to Disney Land with you.'

Liam Dewhurst (9)
Sacred Heart School

MY DOG

My dog barks loudly
When he wants to play.
He growls fiercely
When he is cross.
He whines when he's lonely,
But wags his tail when happy.
I think my dog
Is the best in the world.

Thomas Smith (8)
Sacred Heart School

CHRISTMAS LUNCH

On Christmas Day we eat our lunch
Everything on the table in a huge, huge bunch.
As we start to eat
My heart makes the loudest beat.
Then we bring in the dessert
And if you trip over you might get hurt.

After lunch, I don't know what you're at
If you are inside you might be wearing a hat.
If the boys play with their toys
They keep away the girls.
If the girls wear pearls
They keep the boys away.

Charlotte Edwards (10)
Sacred Heart School

THE FROG

The frog sat on a mossy log
He jumped into
The deep cool pool.
He came back up,
Hopped on the rocks.
I followed him,
I touched him,
He did not fear
Though I came so near.

Katie Trevor (8)
Sacred Heart School

LOOKING OUT OF MY WINDOW

I look out of my window
On a blustery day
And see all those leaves
Which are blowing away.

I watch the bluebird
Sing his song
His bright blue feathers
Ever so long.

Summer and autumn
Pass so fast
Then comes winter
With a mighty blast

The snow is falling
The carpet of white
Covers the garden
You could lose your sight.

Out of my window
You can see the whole year pass,
And I stay stuck to my window
As the year passes fast.

Vicky Lessen (10)
Sacred Heart School

RABBITS

Rabbits are cute and cuddly
They hop and dig all around,
They bounce and skip and jump,
But thump when danger's around.

David Healey (8)
Sacred Heart School

WHAT'S THAT NOISE?

What's that noise coming from the attic?
Maybe a monster with five legs and one eye.
Or could it be a harmless cat,
Waiting for a pat?

The noise is growing louder, bang, bang, tut, tut.
Mum says 'Don't be afraid, you are safe and warm in your cosy bed.'
Mum is just saying that to make me fall asleep.

I'm scared of the noise in the attic.
The monster waiting, mouth watering for a tasty meal.

What's that noise coming from the attic?

Yasmin Houghton-Glasier (11)
Sacred Heart School

POEMS ARE FUN

P oems are really fun to do.
O f course, they are hard too.
E very word can be useful!
M ost poems are beautiful.
S ome are not very well done.

A nd some can be careless.
R eading through the poem books,
E xcellent expression.

F ussy are some
U nder all they are so good.
N ow can we go on to the next one?

Lizzie Haywood (9)
Sacred Heart School

CRAZY DRIVER

I'd love to drive a tractor
Or maybe even a bus,
My mum says I drive her crazy
By making such a fuss.

I'd love to dive a brand new Honda,
Skid and swerve and slide.
I'd love to see some famous people
Or even paraglide.

I'd love to drive at Brand's Hatch,
In a motor car.
I'd even drive a Madaran
Or with a superstar.
Cos I'm a crazy driver.

Kirsty Weddell (9)
Sacred Heart School

THE GIRL NEXT DOOR

The girl next door has six eyes and three legs,
Her hair is made out of five rotten pegs.
Her antennae, I cannot deny,
Reaches up into the sky.
Her hands have suckers on the fingers,
The smell behind her often lingers.
Her nose is long with warts on the end,
But she, I admit is still my best friend!

Alycia Port (11)
Sacred Heart School

ON A CLOUD

I was sitting on the grass one day,
When I saw a cloud drift far away.
The cloud was fluffy, pink and white,
It really was a wonderful sight.
I heard music coming from the cloud,
Then on the cloud I saw angels dance round and round.
Their gold wings so very fair,
As they flew together in the air.
Then a terrible storm came that way,
And washed the little cloud away,
But I shall never forget what I saw that wonderful day.

Emma Donegan (9)
Sacred Heart School

MUNGO AND MAISY

Mungo and Maisy
They'd both drive you crazy
Up and down the wall
Mungo is dopey and Maisy is crazy
Even though they are only small.

Mungo is greedy yet
Maisy is quite speedy
Although they are sweet
If they were calm they'd
Be a treat!

Clementine Hain-Cole (10)
Sacred Heart School

SAILING ALONG THE BLUE SEA

Sailing the blue sea,
Looking for treasure just for me.
Finding an island later that day,
Climbing down the rigging singing hip, hip hooray.
Jumping ashore I found it a bore,
For I knew there was no treasure here,
And there might be pirates who I might fear.
I was sitting under a palm tree eating a banana,
When I saw a shark wrestling a piranha.
I knew the shark would win,
And throw the poor fish in the bin.
Then suddenly something fell on me,
I saw it was a chest and jumped with glee,
And shouted yippee!
That was the day I was sailing along the sea,
(With my treasure next to me).

Oliver Silver (11)
Sacred Heart School

DOLPHINS

Dolphins are lovely creatures,
Splashing, jumping and doing stunts.
Preparing shows for dolphin fans,
People swim, the dolphins they love to join in.
Dolphins skin is very smooth, normally grey or blue.
Dolphins are my favourite animals,
And it will always stay that way.
      Forever.

Zoë Tucker (10)
Sacred Heart School

A FLOOD POEM

A few days ago the water rose to height,
Which gave people a dreadful fright.
As the floods started to spread,
Some people were left without bread.
As the water flowed, everyone moaned
But when they found that the school was closed
They said 'Hip, hip hooray!'
Oh this will be a wonderful day.

They worried as the river was near
But to me it was perfectly clear.
We were on a hill
But still
They worried even more
Like they had before.
The cars couldn't drive
A man was lucky to be alive.
Rain, rain and yet more rain.
As it trickled down the drain,
Oh deary me
More rain I see.
The rain kept on going
As the water was flowing
Some of the river overflowed
Water covered every road.

At last the rain came to an end
Then everything we had to mend!

Eleanor Matthews (10)
Sacred Heart School

THERE WAS A WELSHMAN WHO CAME FROM WALES

There was a Welshman
Who came from Wales
Who ate a bag of carpet nails
Then a saw, then a hammer
Then he ate a giant spanner
Then it stuck down inside
And guess what - he died!

Jessica Morley (10)
Sacred Heart School

HOT AIR BALLOON

Rising up into the sky in a hot air balloon,
People are tiny ants, running and rushing about,
Sheep are still, white dots, sprinkled over fields of green.

Higher we rise to the top of the sky,
Meadows are scattered, green squares,
Dolls' houses are lined along grey roads,
Market places are rectangles of stripy material.

A gust of wind carries us over a city,
Where sky scrapers are miniature towers,
Cars and lorries are millions of insects chasing each other,
A swimming pool of aqua-blue is a block of bright colour,
And rivers are ribbons, whirly, twirly ribbons, leading to grey goldfish
ponds.

Descending down and down, until everything is giant again
And I am a tiny dot in an enormous world.

Abby Higgins (11)
Shinewater Primary School

THE BULL

The bull is the thunder in the dark night sky,
It never stops for anything,
It is the earthquakes that rock the buildings and shake the trees,
If you approach it never wear red, it will charge menacingly at you,
Eyes blazing, ears steaming and feet shaking the ground.

The bull is a steam roller flattening the ground wherever it turns,
It will run through anything to get to its destination,
It is a four-legged devil parting the crowd,
Here's a tip: never go near its young; it will charge fiercely at you,
Tail whipping, head lowering and horns ready to pierce some flesh.

Jason Akehurst (11)
Shinewater Primary School

THE HOWLING WOLF

The howling wolf
Standing in a forest on the hillside,
Howling as if there is no one around him.
But there is.
We can hear him
From the other side of the countryside.
We can hear him
As if he were
The most magnificent hurricane in the world.
But hopefully soon enough he will calm down
And settle down
And go for his midnight feast,
And we can rest until tomorrow.

Lauren Hines (10)
Shinewater Primary School

Rain

I fall all day,
I fall all night.
I flood fields,
I annoy people.
Guess who I am.

I pit-a-pat all day,
I pit-a-pat all night.
I spoil your fun,
I put leaks in your roof.
Guess who I am.

I rain all day,
I rain all night,
And am as wet as the sea.
I fall in drops.
That's right:
I'm the rain.

Craig Badcock (11)
Shinewater Primary School

The Old Owl

As the sun sets an owl awakes.
It is as white as a snowflake.
It sits on its branch like a pile of snow.
The old owl glows white
As it swoops in the dark and misty night.
Looking for a mouse to eat.
But as the sun rises the old owl sleeps.

Joe Buckwell (11)
Shinewater Primary School

KINGS OF THE JUNGLE

I am the King of the jungle.
I'm like the sun shining brightly.
I'm so fast that my prey are like
Tortoises walking.
Some people call me dangerous,
A bully.
But I'm not.
I'm King of the jungle.

I am King of the jungle.
I'm like a bright star
On my own in the black sky
Lighting up the jungle.
Some people call me jealous.
But I'm not.
I'm King of the jungle.

Connor Feeney (10)
Shinewater Primary School

THE CHAMELEON

It is like a storm,
Colour changing,
It is the wind,
Quick, speedy,
It has eyes like tornadoes,
Dots on the tips of spirals,
It is the king of camouflage.

Jimmy Kiteley (10)
Shinewater Primary School

CATS

White cats, black cats,
Lean cats, fat cats,
Come in different shapes and sizes.
New cats, old cats,
Tabby cats, alley cats,
Come in all colours and ages.
Manx cats. Siamese cats,
Brown cats, ginger cats,
Come in all breeds and characters.
Rich cats, poor cats,
Small cats, massive cats,
Some that are longer or smaller than you.
Fierce cats, soft cats,
Kind cats, selfish cats.
I like cats.
Do you?

Kayleigh Fernie (11)
Shinewater Primary School

A STORM

A storm is like an elephant running,
Running very fast.
You can count:
One elephant,
Two elephants,
And you know which way they are coming.
Bug grey elephants with horns,
Horns like lightning.

Sami-Lea Perkins (10)
Shinewater Primary School

BULLY BEARS

I'm a gigantic bear.
A strong, mean bear.
They're just like bullies
Who think they're strong.
I'm a brown, bold thing
As strong as a boulder.
I'm a gigantic bear
And nobody can pull me down.
Bullies they're just like bears.
They say that nobody can get them down.
Bears, they think they're the only strong thing.
Bullies, they're just so mean
Because they're at the top of the school.

Peter Gould (10)
Shinewater Primary School

FISHING FOR A DESTINATION

Down the track you might see
The sports car,
The red sports car,
As fast as a fish.
The fish smells the bait;
The red sports car knows its destination.
The fish turns and swims at 90mph.
The sports car,
The red sports car,
Speeds up
And finally reaches its destination.
And the boy finally catches his first fish.

Jamie Wright (11)
Shinewater Primary School

THE CHASE

Run! Run for your lives!
Help! They're chasing me!
The pride of lions chases the zebra.
The zebra is trapped but the lions don't know
The zebra has a path
A way out.
The zebra runs down that path,
The lions chase the zebra,
The lions kill the zebra.
And if you don't be careful
That might happen to you
By bullies!

Kheva King (10)
Shinewater Primary School

LOOKING OUT THE WINDOW

I'm looking out of my window,
Thinking what I see,
A pretty butterfly
And a bumble-bee.

Flowers are swaying,
With the lovely cool breeze,
I want to smell the daisies,
But I know that I'll sneeze.

I'm looking out my window
I'll tell you what I see,
Pretty butterflies,
And a bumble-bee.

Jade Kearney (11)
Stone Cross School

WHAT HAS HAPPENED TO MY PUPPY?

What has happened to my puppy Mother?
What has happened to my pup?
There is nothing by his basket
But an empty, broken cup.

Why are there muddy paws Mother?
All over the floor,
And an empty basket, where he used to play
Has he gone on a doggy tour?

Why is your face red Mother?
You look so hot and mad.
Please help me find my puppy Mother?
Or I will get really sad.

Suzanna Napper-Page (9)
Stone Cross School

THINGS I WOULD DO IF IT WAS NOT FOR MUM

I would not go to school
Act really cool
I would go out every day
Make a song called 'Swing and Sway.'
Eat loads of junk food
Like people that are rude
Become a rapper
Get a little fatter
Buy a PlayStation 2
Get a cow called Moo.
Have loads of friends
And . . . buy a Mercedes Benz.

Lloyd Francis (10)
Stone Cross School

WHAT HAS HAPPENED TO MY LUNCH BOX TEACHER?

What has happened to my lunchbox Teacher?
What has happened to my lunch?
There's no food in there
But an empty crisp packet with no crunch.

Why is my lid wide open?
Right splat on the floor?
Why is nobody at the trolley?
Why is nobody at the door?

Why don't you tell me Teacher?
I can keep a secret well,
But why are you so silent?
Because my chocolate I can smell.

Where is it then Teacher?
It smells like it's in your hair.
Have you eaten it Miss?
Maybe you did it for a dare.

I still feel hungry Miss
I haven't got anything to munch
What has happened to my lunchbox Teacher?
What has happened to my lunch?

Victoria Ball (9)
Stone Cross School

WHAT HAPPENED TO . . .

What happened to the picture?
What happened to the picture?
There's nothing on the wall
All bar the fixture.

Why is there glass on the floor Mother?
Underneath where the picture used to be?
Just a dirty mark left on the wall
Now I wonder where it can be.

Georgina Haffenden (10)
Stone Cross School

THIS IS HAGRID

This is Hagrid
That has the coat
That has loads of pockets

This is Hagrid
That has the coat
That has loads of pockets
And took Harry Potter to Diagon Alley

This is Hagrid
That has the coat
That has loads of pockets
And took Harry to Gringots
To get some money
And took Harry to Diagon Alley
To buy his robes, wand and magical stuff.

This is Hagrid
That has the coat
That has loads of pockets
And took Harry to Gringots
To get some money.
And took Harry to Diagon Alley
To buy his robes, wand and magical stuff.
To go to Hogwarts.

Matthew Golledge (9)
Stone Cross School

Dare Wake The Dead

If you dare to go to the graveyard,
At midnight, when the moon is full,
Be careful not to go alone,
Or else you'll be in Dracula's zone.

You'll hear the terrifying *creak*
Of coffins. As the dead come to life.
And the wind howling from the trees makes you shudder,
So don't be scared to leap.

You'll hear the scream of the dead going walking,
Through the graveyard, cold and bleak.
You'll feel the touch of ghostly spirits,
On your skin that'll make you freak.

You'll smell the odour of flesh rotting,
You'll see the angel and Grim Reaper fighting over the dead.
As you run desperately to sprint to the church door,
To escape the curse of the dead.

Thomas Sharp (9)
Stone Cross School

What Has Happened To Mum?

What has happened to Mum, Father?
What has happened to Mum?
I've looked at the table Father
And all that's left is a bread crumb.

Why have I got no breakfast, Father?
My tummy's started rumbling
You keep on talking to yourself, Father
What are you mumbling?

Why are you doing the housework, Father?
Making the place tidy and neat
Why do you say you're far too busy
Even to make me a bite to eat.

Why do you keep on visiting the hospital, Father?
And leaving me alone?
I really miss her, Father
When is Mother coming home?

Aimeé Read (10)
Stone Cross School

WHAT HAS HAPPENED TO JAMIE?

What has happened to Jamie Mother?
What has happened to Jay?
On the window there's a blood stain,
No matter how I wash it, it never goes away.
Why did I hear a slash last night Mother,
And a voice suddenly halt?
But you say it is nothing but the heating vault.
I heard an engine roar Mother and a person scream
Also his money box is broken
But you say it was just a dream.
Why do you wander the house Mother,
Looking for a place to hide?
This always happens when a police car passes by.
Why every night do you cry Mother?
And why does the curtain flap free?
What has happened to Jamie Mother,
That you pretend not to see?

Jamie Segwagwe (10)
Stone Cross School

THIS IS THE STONE

This is the stone

This is the stone
Hidden by chambers

This is the stone
Hidden by chambers
Under the trapdoor

This is the stone
Hidden by chambers
Under the stiff trapdoor
Guarded by Fluffy

This is the stone
Hidden by chambers
Under the stiff trapdoor
Guarded by Fluffy
In the third floor corridor

This is the stone
Hidden by chambers
Under the stiff trapdoor
Guarded by Fluffy
In the third floor corridor
Of Hogwarts school

This is the stone
Hidden by chambers
Under the stiff trapdoor
Guarded by Fluffy
In the third floor corridor
Of Hogwarts school
Which Harry Potter was sent to.

Caitlin Rowson (10)
Stone Cross School

WHAT HAS HAPPENED TO PUSSY?

What has happened to Pussy, Mum?
What has happened to the cat?
She might have fallen off the roof, Mum,
I hope she didn't go splat!

What's that flying outside, Mum?
Why is it wearing a hat?
Why has it got 'S' on its chest, Mum?
I think it's Super Cat!

It's definitely not Super Cat, Mum,
I was just imagining things.
Why is there a knock at the door, Mum?
And why does the doorbell ring?

Who is the man at the door, Mum?
Why is the cat on his head?
So Pussy didn't go splat, Mum?
She is safe, she is not dead!

Jonathan Riches (10)
Stone Cross School

THIS IS THE BROOMSTICK

This is the broomstick.

This is the broomstick,
That held Harry Potter

This is the broomstick,
That held Harry Potter
When he plays Quidditch.

This is the broomstick,
That held Harry Potter
When he plays Quidditch.
And its make is Nimbus 2000,

This is the broomstick,
That held Harry Potter
When he plays Quidditch.
And its make is Nimbus 2000,
That bent the first year rule.

This is the broomstick,
That held Harry Potter
When he plays Quidditch.
And its make is Nimbus 2000,
That bent the first year rule.
Which Harry Potter practised on.

This is the broomstick,
That held Harry Potter
When he plays Quidditch.
And its make is Nimbus 2000,
That bent the first year rule.
Which Harry Potter practised on,
So he could win Quidditch matches.

This is the broomstick,
That held Harry Potter
When he plays Quidditch.
And its make is Nimbus 2000,
That bent the first year rule.
Which Harry Potter practised on,
So he could win Quidditch matches,
Which he did by catching the snitch.

Craig Bartlett (9)
Stone Cross School

WHAT HAS HAPPENED TO . . . ?

What has happened to the kitten Mother?
What has happened to the kitten?
There is nothing in the basket Mother
Except for an old mitten.

The cat-flap is open Mother
Flapping, flapping free
Just a set of muddy paw prints
That lead towards the tree.

Why do you not answer me Mother?
I can hear a meowing from the tree
Why don't you get a ladder
And go and see?

It is him Mother?
I can't believe I missed him so.

Stephanie Tween (9)
Stone Cross School

HAGRID'S COAT

These are the mice.

These are the mice,
That live in Hagrid's coat

These are the mice,
That live in Hagrid's coat
That ate the cake

These are the mice,
That live in Hagrid's coat
That ate the cake
That was made for Harry Potter

These are the mice,
That live in Hagrid's coat
That ate the cake
That was made for Harry Potter
The day it was his birthday.

These are the mice,
That live in Hagrid's coat
That ate the cake
That was made for Harry Potter
The day it was his birthday.
Who ate the coat pocket

These are the mice,
That live in Hagrid's coat
That ate the cake
That was made for Harry Potter
The day it was his birthday.
Who ate the coat pocket
Who escaped to Harry's room.

These are the mice,
That live in Hagrid's coat
That ate the cake
That was made for Harry Potter
The day it was his birthday.
Who ate the coat pocket
Who escaped to Harry's room.
That screamed through Hogwarts School.

Jack Davies (10)
Stone Cross School

WHAT HAS HAPPENED TO ASHLEY?

What has happened to Ashley Mother?
What has happened to Ash?
I looked in the large bin
But found a piece of trash.

Why is the front door open?
The net curtains flapping free?
And there's a circle on the dusty desk
Where his football used to be.

Where has he gone Mother?
And where is his bike?
I've looked everywhere
So maybe he's gone on a hike.

I woke to cries this morning
I heard a bike go ding
Then came silence
Followed by the phone ring.

Liam Hughes (9)
Stone Cross School

MUMMY STORY

This is the man.

This is the man
That found the door
That led to the tomb.

This is the man
That found the door
That led to the tomb
Of Tutankhamun.

This is the man
That found the door
That led to the tomb
Of Tutankhamun,
And unleashed the curse
Of the pharaoh king.

This is the curse.

This is the curse
That killed the man
Who found the door
That led to the tomb
Of Tutankhamun.

This is the mummy.

This is the mummy
That found the door
That led to the tomb
Of Tutankhamun
To scare the men
Out of their wits.

These are the scissors!

These are the scissors
That saved the men!

Natasha Henson (9)
Stone Cross School

WHAT HAS HAPPENED TO MY FISH?

What has happened to my fish Mother?
What has happened to my fish?
There's nothing in this house except his castle
And beside it an empty cat dish.

Why is the water out Mother?
And the floor's all wet.
The food's all gone and in its place a china doll.
He watched you pay your debts.

Why do you turn your head Mother?
Why does the cat not eat?
And why do you wash the floor Mother?
And cover the tank with a sheet?

I woke to a cat being sick Mother
I heard a fish flap.
Why do you say the things I heard
Were the cat scratching on the mat?

I heard a box open Mother
And something drop
But now I ask you Mother
That you said you sold it to the shop.

Jasmine Redfern (9)
Stone Cross School

WHERE DO ALL THE MONKEYS GO?

Where do all the monkeys go,
When they're in the lively zoo?
Do they live in houses?
And do they go to a posh loo?

Do they wear clothes Mother?
Do they watch TV?
And do they blink?
And can they see?

Do they have friends like you and me?
Have they got sisters or brothers?
And were they ever human?
And do they have mothers?

Do they know how to spell?
Do they do things wrong?
Are they frightened?
And do they sing songs?

Did they ever read books?
Did they ever have greens?
Did they make a noise?
Did they ever wear jeans?

I will go to the zoo today
And see what they do
And put it in a poem,
And you can read it too.

Joanne Mitchell (10)
Stone Cross School

THIS IS THE BOY

This is the boy.

This is the boy
Called Harry Potter

This is the boy
Called Harry Potter
Who looked in the mirror

This is the boy
Called Harry Potter
Who looked in the mirror
Who saw his parents

This is the boy
Called Harry Potter
Who looked in the mirror
Who saw his parents
Who talked to his parents

This is the boy
Called Harry Potter
Who looked in the mirror
Who saw his parents
Who talked to his parents
Who went to bed

This is the boy
Called Harry Potter
Who looked in the mirror
Who saw his parents
Who talked to his parents
Who went to bed
Who fell asleep.

Zoe McCue (10)
Stone Cross School

THIS IS THE CENTAUR

This is the centaur.

This is the centaur,
That heard the cry,

This is the centaur,
That heard the cry,
That helped Harry,

This is the centaur,
That heard the cry,
That helped Harry,
That took him from danger,

This is the centaur,
That heard the cry,
That helped Harry,
That took him from danger,
That took him to Hagrid,

This is the centaur,
That heard the cry,
That helped Harry,
That took him from danger,
That took him to Hagrid,
Who says 'Mars is bright tonight.'

This is the centaur,
That heard the cry,
That helped Harry,
That took him from danger,
That took him to Hagrid,
Who says 'Mars is bright tonight.'
Who has a hairy back.

Ryan-Neil Linley (10)
Stone Cross School

WHAT HAS HAPPENED TO MAISY?

What has happened to Maisy, Mother?
What has happened to Mais?
There's nothing in her bed, Mother
Where she used to lay and gaze.

Why is the door wide open, Mother?
And the house feels so cold,
I wonder where Maisy is, Mother
She wasn't very old.

Why do you turn your head, Mother?
And why do tear-drops fall?
I really want to know, Mother
I'm left with nothing at all.

Ben Boobier (9)
Stone Cross School

WHAT'S HAPPENED TO MY DOG?

What's happened to my dog?
What's happened to my dog Dad?
I've looked everywhere
He was such a great lad.

Look at the hole in the fence Dad,
Look at the hole in the fence.
Maybe we could put up a reward,
For at least fifty pence.

Why did you turn away Dad?
Why did you turn away?
Now he's gone
This is where he used to lay.

Jack Kenward (9)
Stone Cross School

THE THINGS I'D DO IF IT WEREN'T FOR MUM

If it weren't for Mum I'd:

Live on Coke, crisps but never caviar,
Trade the fish for a tarantula.
Lay in front of the telly,
Only wash when I'm really smelly.
Leave a horrible sight everywhere,
Play loud music, jump from here to there.
Paint my room green and black,
Leave the videos in a stack.
Do a competition, be a runner-up,
And score a goal to win the World Cup.
Find out what it's like to be me,
Let this list grow long and get free.

PS Take my savings in my hand,
Buy a ticket for a lifetime trip to Lego Land!

Matthew Winter (10)
Stone Cross School

TEN THINGS YOU FIND IN MY DOG'S BASKET

My dad's dressing gown belt.
An old chewed cushion.
A teddy with no face.
A dog-hair infested blanket.
Last week's leftovers.
A soaking wet, squeaky pig.
A mud pool, toy lamb.
A new chew bone.
An old burst football.
And last but not least . . .
My racing cap.

Cleo Jones (10)
Stone Cross School

160

WHAT'S HAPPENED TO MY CAT MUM?

What's happened to my cat Mum?
What's happened to my cat?
She is not in my bedroom Mum.
She is not on her mat.

Have you let her out Mum?
Has she gone through her flap?
Has she gone and run away
With another cat?

Why did she run away Mum?
Why did she run away?
Is it because she never liked me,
Or because I would never play?

Sarah-Louise McAllister (9)
Stone Cross School

WHAT HAS HAPPENED TO MY PE KIT?

What has happened to my PE kit?
What has happened to my kit?
I've looked on my peg Miss
Maybe someone's eaten it.

I found my empty bag Miss
Dropped down onto the floor
I thought I saw a glimpse of it
Running out through the door.

I followed it all through the door,
Followed it all the way.
You'll never guess who was wearing it Miss
My best friend Lucy, Miss.

Leanne Howells (10)
Stone Cross School

IN THE GRAVEYARD

In a graveyard

In a graveyard
you will find

In a graveyard
you will find
a ten-headed demon

In a graveyard
you will find
a ten-headed demon
a blood-sucking werewolf

In a graveyard
you will find
a ten-headed demon
a blood-sucking werewolf
a three-eyed ghost

In a graveyard
you will find
a ten-headed demon
a blood-sucking werewolf
a three-eyed ghost
a zombie with no head

In a graveyard
you will find
a ten-headed demon
a blood-sucking werewolf
a three-eyed ghost
a zombie with no head
and one-eyed humans.

And if you go there you're doomed.

Robyn Juniper
Stone Cross School

FAIRGROUND STORY

This is the boy.

This is the boy,
Who went to the fair.

This is the boy,
Who went to the fair,
To go on a ride.

This is the boy,
Who went to the fair,
To go on a ride,
To have some fun.

This is the boy,
Who went to the fair,
To go on a ride,
To have some fun
With his friends
But he was sick!

This was the friend
That had sick in his lap
From the boy
Who went to the fair
To go on a ride
To have some fun
With his friends
But he had to go home!

Zoë Durrant (9)
Stone Cross School

THINGS I'D DO IF IT WEREN'T FOR DAD

Watch telly my way (really loudly)
Make loads of noise
Eat lots of food
Take my sister's toys!

Stay in bed
Play games all day
Make people do
Whatever I say!

Take people's things
Make them mine
Do what I want
Waste loads of time!

Leave my homework
Buy new pets
Play outside
Even when it's wet!

Buy new clothes
Call my best friend
Drive my sister
Round the bend!

Play with my hair
Paint my bedroom a lovely gold
Make my sister do
As she is told!

Rosanne Field (10)
Stone Cross School

THE FOOTBALL COACH'S DAY IN BED

Our football coach is having a day in bed,
He's sent his pets to training instead.
There's . . . a parrot to read the register,
    A kangaroo to make the teams fair,
    An orang-utan to watch over the game
    A lion to shout encouragement.
Oh and a cat and dog to support them.
I bet you never knew just how much a coach can do.

Our players are having a day in bed,
They've sent their pets to training instead.
There's . . . A dog to make mistakes
    A cat to fall asleep
I bet you never knew just how little a player can do.

Amy Steele (9)
Stone Cross School

WHAT DO TEACHERS DO AFTER SCHOOL?

Do they . . .

Go and doze off and watch telly all day?
Or maybe they will go and have a little play.
They could be chasing their mysterious cats,
Or would they rather have a chit-chat?
They could stuff themselves with chocolates and cakes
And ten minutes later their tummies would ache.
They could be up cooking tea
Or they could be swimming in the sea.
Maybe they will be off on a plane
Up and away to sunny Spain.
They could be off to the gym
So they can get very slim.

Ashley Ratcliffe (10)
Stone Cross School

WINTER

When you walk on the snow it goes crunch,
The robins fly high in the sky,
Playing in the snow and make snowballs,
With your friends and throw them high.

When you go out and start to shiver,
Icicles hang from the window ledge,
There is frost on the ground in the park,
You can ride down a hill on a sledge.

You can make snowmen with loads of snow,
At night snowflakes fall in the sky,
The car is frosty and cold in the morning,
And over the snowflakes lie.

Pascale McIlwaine (9)
The Fold School

FIREWORKS

Fireworks are fun
Fireworks are pretty
Fireworks are bright
Fireworks are beautiful
Colourful
Dashing rockets.

Whizzing
Round and round
Sparkling colours,
Bonfire loving
Bonfire blazing
Bonfire spitting.

Hannah Briggs (8)
The Fold School

THE SNAKE

The snake, that slimy thing
Sliding up the trees through leaves
The animals watch it go by
Looking for its prey.
Orange and green the colour of its scaly skin
It's slivering, in the jungle hiding behind trees
Putting it's head high
Looking up to the sky
Winter comes
It's hiding in a dark cave
Too cold outside
The trees are covered with snow
No hunters in the forest
No killers in the trees
Spring comes
His eggs are laid
The snake comes out to play
The sun is shining today.

Benjamin Hickey (8)
The Fold School

DOLPHINS

D   olphins are lovely, gentle animals,
O   ver rocks, the dolphins jump flipping their fins,
L   Leaping out of the sparkling water,
P   lease don't kill the dolphins.
H   elp the dolphins so they won't be caught,
I   n the sea, the dolphins are in danger.
N   one of the dolphins can harm you, please don't harm them.

Alice Boyle (6)
The Fold School

THE BUTTERFLY

Hello little butterfly.
How you flutter.
How you fly.
Come rest upon my buttercup.
Rest your wings, sleep, curl up.
How you flutter over my head,
The colour of your wings orange and red.
So delicate you little thing.
Don't fly too fast,
Don't crumple your wing.
How they hunt you down like prey.
How they simply ruin your day.
How they put you on display,
How they spoil your fun with play.

Ben Sa-Hutchings (10)
The Fold School

DOLPHINS

D   olphins swimming through the sea
O   ver rocks and swimming on
L   eaping out of the water
P   lease don't kill the dolphins
H   appy creatures play all day
I   love dolphins in every way
N   one of them have hurt you
S   wimming high and low.

Christie Mudie (9)
The Fold School

MY HAMSTER

H is for Hurbert which is my hamsters name.
U is for understanding my friend.
R is for running round in his wheel.
B is for burying his food in his house.
E is for eyes so blue and bright.
R is for rummaging around in his cage at night.
T is for twitching his nose in the air.

H is for hair so soft on his back.
A is for animal so tiny and sweet.
M is for mouse-like features that he has.
S is for scuttling around in his cage.
T is for treats which he is so fond of.
E is for ears always listening for me.
R is rattling his cage for me.

This is what Hurbert means to me.
I love him lots and lots.

Lara Kiziltuna (8)
The Fold School

DOLPHINS

D own in the deep sea the dolphins play,
O ver and under the sparkling waves.
L eaping up and down over the glistening sea,
P erfect, pretty sight that they give me.
H arbour boats start going out to sea,
I n danger the dolphins, they are calling for me.
N o one should harm the beautiful creatures,
S tand still and watch their beautiful features.

Charlotte Morris (8)
The Fold School

WHALES

W hales are lovely amazing creatures,
H ow they like to swim in the sea,
A lso they have interesting features
L et them live and be free
E veryone watches them from the beaches,
S ometimes we have to let them be.

Bonnie Carroll (8)
The Fold School

A TOUCH OF FROST

As you walk through the frosted trees
Crunching leaves, cracking ice.
As you tread through the frosted wood
Shivering frost, mysterious mist
Think of dew dropping petals on roses
Wild sunset crisped grass.
Think of robins hovering above the ice
Trapped bubbles, ice cold water.
Look through the valley; you can see translucent mist,
Haunted mist. Spikes settle on leaves.
Think of frost twinkling on tips of grass
Sparks of frost, glittering spikes.
The gleaming fiery sun shining
Above the valley's trees
Blue sky, long shadows.

As the mist slowly drifts away,
A brand new day awaits
Jack Frost.

Claire Petzal (10)
Vinehall Preparatory School

A WALK AROUND VINEHALL IN AUTUMN

The sound of screaming, eager, conker-loving children searching for wooden gobstoppers, football-sized conkers under the dense, dim, green trees like in the night.

The sight of a silvery-clear, broken glass web stretched between three pieces of dewy, freshly-mown, crisp, emerald grass on a sloping, tree-infested hill like a slithering snake.

The feel of the soggy, squelchy, boggy mud in the softish, damp, everlasting ground next to a stretched, medieval crumbling wall.

The smell of the draughty, chilly, free-flying air on a breezy, bright humid day in a cold, brisk, vapouristic month.

The taste of a dry-blood, arid, dwarf-sized blackberry on a spindly, uneven, ruined branch of a prehistoric, battered, wiry tree.

Christopher Doherty (10)
Vinehall Preparatory School

THE WATER'S LIFE

Gleaming, rushing
Through the pitted reef,
Up to the surface
Gurgling with glee
To reach the sky
Down comes the rain
Like machine gun fire,
What a sight!
Raining silver sky.

Ben Reeve (11)
Vinehall Preparatory School

A Walk Around Vinehall On An Autumn Day

I saw a long, light green river of grass slithering down a dark lime-coloured hill covered with dew, sparkling in the morning sun, like an endless slimy emerald snake.

I saw an old wall winding its way round the school with roots and plants growing out of it, like millions of worms that have just hatched eager to see the outside world.

I saw huge stretching clouds floating over the lovely light blue sky, like candy floss on its way to be eaten up by the sparkling bright yellow sun.

I heard the whistle of a dark blue train on its way to Robertsbridge Station just visible through the morning mist, like a puff of smoke in the air.

I heard red-chested happy robins singing their early morning song in the morning mist.

I heard excited children when they had just found a great conker in the wet pea-green grass.

I smelt lovely cold fresh air floating round me like a light wind following me around my walk round the school grounds.

I smelt the new autumn flowers floating around me like they were telling me that they were there.

I smelt the new autumn, juicy blackberries dangling from the pea-green holly bush like millions of bouncy balls trying to escape from the bush.

I tasted the sweet and sour blackberries that were hanging desperately from the lime-green holly bush.

I tasted the new fresh air blowing around me like a swoosh of air that you feel when something goes past you really quickly.

I tasted some hot chocolate when I had just come in from outside in the cold and I was freezing, it was like a sudden gush of warm blood shooting through my body.

I felt a cold wet green wine bottle that was covered in dew all over, all white and easy to just wipe away to make it clean like a brand new cloth sweeping over the dew.

I felt a fresh blackberry on a bush all squidgy and soft like squelching mud in a flooded football pitch.

I felt green grass under my feet drowned with dew like a small pathetic boat in a rough dark blue ocean swaying round helplessly calling for help.

Jack Tucker (10)
Vinehall Preparatory School

A LIGHT SUMMER SHOWER

A warm, humid, summer's day,
The sun shining, casting a ray,
As tiny droplets, sting your face,
Raindrops shiver, shout and chase,
At the busy moving of the town,
Umbrellas rise,
Turning the urban streets dark brown,
Birds, gently sway their wings,
As the array of light begins to sting.

Then even the grasses, on the dune,
Play no more their reedy tune,
The pale colouring brightly changes,
To the same misty blue, in the usual ranges,
Umbrellas steadily close up,
As the birds give a sign, 'the rain has come to a stop!'
The light summer's shower, repeating its routine,
And carefully, caringly, washing the green . . .

Rebecca Wingrad (11)
Vinehall Preparatory School

A Walk Around Vinehall On An Autumn Morning

Orange-yellow and also green tufts of freshly dyed sheep's' wool,
The green is the colour of dark, wet crocodile skin
Swaying in the light, fresh breeze
Standing out against the icy light-blue sky.
The sky looks as though it has just come back from the laundry.
The spiky, slippery, wet grass covering the grounds,
With a light strip running through the middle where it has been mowed,
Looks like an emerald river winding through the country.
A tiny, fluffy, cuddly bunny rabbit sitting with his big pointy ears
Pricked up for listening predators.

A loud, long bellowing horn like an enormous brass, shiny trumpet
                               booming out into the morning.
Coming from a long, fast, snaky train which whizzes past,
Carrying people to different places disturbing the lovely calm stillness
Of the fresh new morning.
The sound of the birds twittering along in chorus,
Whistling a tune of happiness and freedom.
The sound of the faint light breeze whispering through the trees,
It makes the air nice and cool.

The smell of the big round juicy blackberries,
Drifting through the air,
The smell of lovely perfumes all mixed up together.
When you breathe in, the smell of cold air wafts in
Through your chilled icy nose.
If it has been a cold crispy day when you come in
You smell a lovely roast dinner cooking for you
And you feel a warm rush through you

Excitement rushes through you when you look for the best conkers,
Then you see it lying in the wet, crispy bed of leaves glowing,
A huge shiny slippery conker waiting to be found.
When you step outside a sudden chill catches your warm body,
But then you feel the glorious, hot sun beating against your cheek.

The taste of the big round blackberries juicy and sweet.
The taste of hot chocolate rushing down your throat after being outside.

Claudia Weston (10)
Vinehall Preparatory School

A MYSTICAL WORLD OF FROST

As I run outside,
I am in a whole new world.
I dance through the shimmering grass,
And rub my finger over a frost-rimmed branch.
I am in a world of frost,
Glittering, glimmering, shimmering frost.
As I peer out into the distance,
I shiver, looking over the haunting shadows.
I breathe out and suddenly I'm a frost princess,
Surrounded by my crisp frosty breath.
I tiptoe along to the pond,
Where I pick up a piece of glassy ice.
Suddenly, I am in a ballroom,
Drinking from an icy glass,
With ghosts dancing all around me.
I admire the icy fountain,
With glittering, sparkling ice,
Twinkling, like a star in the sky.
Suddenly, I'm holding a frosty star,
And I float up into the dead of night,
Away, into the sky.

Emma May (10)
Vinehall Preparatory School

VINEHALL IN AUTUMN

I can see a glittering, shining spider web like a silver net.
I see a long, light, crisp green road stretch over the hill and out of sight
among the dark, green, blobby bushes.
A shiny, glittering conker as it sits there upon the damp, dewy grass
waiting to be found.

I can hear the crispy crunch of newly laid gravel like a great, greasy
monster crunching and munching white, succulent, crispy
bones in his damp, dark moist lair.
The happy twittering birds as they sit in the damp, dark, cool,
shady tree.
The snapping, crackling, crisp sound as I walk on the rotting, damp,
cold twigs.

I can smell the fresh, new, original autumn air on my frozen face and
skin as I walk on the cool, damp, moist grass.
The squelchy, disgusting, horrible smell of the moist, wet, terrible mud.
The smell of the warm, sweet, lovely classroom as I enter out of the
Pounding, torrential, blowing rain like a huge, great, awesome
hurricane.

I can taste the sweet, rich, juiciness of gorgeous, scrumptious, succulent
blackberries that can be used instead of face paint.
The new, fresh, original autumn's air blowing on my face like a
vacuum cleaner on reverse.
The taste of the sweet, warm, fragrant smell of the warmish, kind,
loving classroom as I enter out of the cold, freezing, damp autumn.

I can feel the smooth, shiny, glassy surface of a damp, cold,
dewy conker.
The damp, moist, humid dew on the crispy, emerald green grass.

Nicholas Weston-Smith (10)
Vinehall Preparatory School

A WINTER MORNING

Brightly glimmering frost sits
On the branches of trees,
Silhouetted against the misty background.

At the pond,
Icy crystals glittering on the surface,
The sun's faint rays
Coming through the trees making murky reflections
Peer up from the depths.

Far off,
The mist hangs suspended in the air,
Making the rays of the sun
Shine eerily on the miniature icicles
Of frost sticking up
Out of the grass.

Children run,
Screaming with laughter
Over this
Cruel, icy frost,
Slipping on melted mud.
They take leaves off trees
And crunch them in their hands,
Delighted at the crackling sound.
But this wonderful atmosphere
Will have disappeared by midday,
Only to come back
Next morning.

Ben Huntington-Rainey (10)
Vinehall Preparatory School

A WINTER'S MORNING

As I step outside into the coolness of the winter's morn
I see layers of suspended mist,
Silhouettes of bare trees,
I follow the slowly disappearing frost,
Gaze entranced at small snow crystals on the evergreens,
Stepping on crunchy leaves, frost resting on the veins.
The trees shudder in the winter wind.
I feel the wind's wrath,
I step into the warmth of the school
And glance out at the trees,
The trees waiting for spring.

Olivia Jeffes (9)
Vinehall Preparatory School

WATER

Angry, splashing raindrops on the roof
The sun slips shyly from behind a cloud
A rainbow arches her glory,
Shimmering in the pale sun
The clouds drift forward,
Skies darken,
On ominous slate grey,
The bright light's gone.

Madeleine Barnes (11)
Vinehall Preparatory School